VAN GOGH

A BEGINNER'S GUIDE

ANDREW FORREST

Hodder & Stoughton

A MEMBER OF THE HODDER HEADLINE GROUP

DEDICATION

For Margaret

ACKNOWLEDGEMENTS

I should like to thank my parents, friends, colleagues and students for their support and forbearance during the writing of this book. Particular thanks are due to Anita Vriend, Librarian at the Van Gogh Museum, Amsterdam, for her generous assistance with new sources of information and for answering questions that arose during my research.

Orders: please contact Bookpoint Ltd, 130 Milton Park, Abingdon, Oxon OX14 4SB. Telephone: (44) 01235 827720, Fax: (44) 01235 400454. Lines are open from 9.00–6.00, Monday to Saturday, with a 24-hour message answering service. Email address: orders@bookpoint.co.uk

British Library Cataloguing in Publication Data
A catalogue record for this title is available from The British Library

ISBN 0 340 84619 4

First published 2002
Impression number   10 9 8 7 6 5 4 3 2 1
Year   2008 2007 2006 2005 2004 2003 2002

Copyright © 2002 Andrew Forrest

Cover photo from Archivo Iconographico, S.A./Corbis
Illustration 1, 2, and 4 from AKG London
Illustration 3 from AKG London/Erich Lessing

Typeset by Transet Limited, Coventry, England.
Printed in Great Britain for Hodder & Stoughton Educational, a division of Hodder Headline Plc, 338 Euston Road, London NW1 3BH by Cox & Wyman, Reading, Berks.

CONTENTS

Van Gogh's garden,
54 rue Lepic
Montmartre.

Author's drawing (1991) of courtyard at 54 Rue Lepic, Paris, where Vincent van Gogh lodged, June 1886–February 1888.

Foreword

GUIDE TO SOURCES IN THE TEXT

The correspondence of Vincent van Gogh is quoted from two sources throughout this book.

1 The 1958 English translation of *The Complete Letters of Vincent van Gogh*, edited by J. van Gogh-Bonger and V. W. van Gogh, and translated by J. van Gogh-Bonger and C. de Dood. This three-volume translation was published by Thames and Hudson in London in 1958 and reprinted in 2000.

2 The more recent concise edition, *The Letters of Vincent van Gogh*, selected and edited by Ronald de Leeuw and translated by Arnold Pomerans was published by Penguin Classics in Harmondsworth in 1996. This selection re-translated the letters into English and re-dated some of them.

A number was assigned to each letter in the Van Gogh correspondence in the 1958 edition, and this numbering system was retained in the 1996 concise edition.

Please note that where the quotations are from the three-volume 1958 edition, this is indicated in the text by the letter number. Where the quotations are from the 1996 edition, this is indicated in the text by the letter number and an asterisk.

Letters preceded by 'L' were from Vincent to Theo van Gogh unless otherwise stated in this book.

Those preceded by 'R' were to Anthon van Rappard.

Those preceded by 'W' were to Vincent's sister Willemina ('Wil').

Those preceded by 'B' were to Emile Bernard.

Those preceded by 'T' were from Theo to Vincent van Gogh.

Quotations in Chapter 6, apart from the letters, are taken from *Van Gogh: A Retrospective*, edited by Susan Alyson Stein, published by Könemann, Cologne, 1986.

Where other works on van Gogh are referred to, the authors' names are given in the main body of the text, with full details in the Further Reading section of this book.

Vincent – a Life

CHILDHOOD AND EARLY EDUCATION, MARCH 1853–MARCH 1868

What's in a name? Vincent Willem were forenames bestowed on four members of the Van Gogh family, three of whom became involved in art. The most famous was Vincent, the artist (1853–90), but there was also his uncle who was an art dealer (1820–88), and his nephew (1889–78), founder of the Van Gogh Museum in Amsterdam. Vincent himself was named after a stillborn brother who died in 1852, exactly one year before his own birth.

Vincent, the artist, was the eldest of six surviving children born to Theodorus (called Dorus) and Anna van Gogh in the Dutch province of North Brabant. His commitment to art, nature and the written word and, for a time, to zealous Christianity were related to the interests and careers of his family. In fact, no less than three of Vincent's uncles, as well as his brother Theo, were art dealers, while a cousin by marriage, Anton Mauve, was a landscape painter. Vincent's father was a bibliophile and a minister in the Dutch Reformed (Protestant) Church, while his mother, an avid letter writer, was a skilled amateur artist and naturalist. Vincent's own love and detailed understanding of nature also derived from the countryside where he was born; he was to spend the first 16 years of his life in and around his birthplace, Zundert, close to the woods and rich farmland of North Brabant.

It was in Zundert, at the age of seven, that Vincent first attended school. However, a drunken teacher and unruly classmates caused Vincent's parents to take him away. From then on Vincent's schooling was erratic, but never his love of learning. After three years of home tuition, Vincent returned to school, aged 11. It was here, at the Zevenbergen boarding school, that his talent for languages was encouraged. At his final school, the Willem II state secondary school in Tilburg, which he attended from September 1866 to March 1868, Vincent's flair for art became more apparent. Unfortunately, perhaps because of financial or health reasons, he had to leave before his fifteenth birthday. Throughout his education, Vincent showed academic prowess (he was near the top of the class at Tilburg) and his passion for literature stayed with him forever. Having left school, he now had time on his hands to read widely and to contemplate the future.

SELLING ART AT GOUPIL'S, JULY 1869–APRIL 1876

Long before he became an artist in the early 1880s, Vincent van Gogh was working within the art trade, a profession he came to know intimately, although never to great financial advantage. Ultimately, his career as an artist scaled the heights of genius, whereas his career as an art dealer spiralled into decline.

In the beginning, everything went well. Vincent was apprenticed to **Goupil & Company's** chain of art galleries and did well at their prestigious Hague branch for nearly four years. Although he was far from home, he was able to board with family friends, the Roos family and he often visited his Aunt Fie and her daughter Jet. The Hague branch of Goupil's was patronized by the Dutch royal family and Vincent got to know **The Hague School** artists, such as Anton Mauve, who would later marry into Vincent's family and become his art tutor. Vincent began as a clerical trainee at Goupil's and then, having learnt the necessary 'people skills', he moved on to selling photographs of paintings by Salon artists like Meissonier and more 'modern' artists like Millet (both

KEYWORDS

Goupil & Co.: international firm of art dealers, later known as Boussod & Valadon. Vincent was employed in their branches in The Hague, London and Paris (1869–76).

The Hague School: flourished between c.1860 and 1900. The group specialized in atmospheric landscapes and beach scenes but also painted views of town and city. Apart from Anton Mauve, the School also included Jozef Israëls ('the Dutch Millet').

Meissonier and Millet were heroes of Vincent). Clients and artists alike thought highly of Vincent and, when he left The Hague branch in May

1873, his boss Hermanus Tersteeg described him as 'the diligent studious youth'.

Next, Vincent was promoted from The Hague to Goupil's London branch, where he remained for 16 months (see Chapter 3). At this stage, he still returned home for holidays with his family at Helvoirt, his father's new parish. However, it was during this time that Vincent received an emotional blow. He had fallen in love, but his love was not returned; what was joy, now turned to sorrow. Until recently this woman was thought to have been Vincent's landlady's daughter, Eugenie Loyer or perhaps even the landlady herself, Ursula. However, recent research suggests that it may have been his second cousin, Carolien Haanebeek, with whom he was in love. Vincent became depressed and withdrawn, and started to take refuge in religion. Hoping to cheer up his nephew, Uncle Cent engineered a temporary transfer for Vincent to Goupil's Paris branch (October to December 1874). Vincent then returned to London, but he had only been back five months, when Goupil's recalled him to Paris in May 1875 – his fourth move in five years. His resentment at being moved about was palpable. Rude to clients and no longer the smart employee, Vincent preferred reading in his garret to 'customer care' at Goupil's. His spirit was elsewhere, fired by reading the Bible or by looking at treasures in the Louvre. Dismissal from the firm came on 1 April 1876, when Vincent was just 23.

With experience of working in three capital cities for the largest firm of art dealers in Europe, what had gone wrong in Vincent's professional life? His employers were grand, yet clearly he himself lacked commitment. The immediate cause of his dismissal from Goupil's in Paris was his wish to spend Christmas 1875 in Holland, with his family. He had wanted to see how they were settling in after their new move from Helvoirt to Etten, quite near his home town of Zundert, but recklessly he had not sought permission to absent himself from work. No firm could let this pass.

Although this marked the end of Vincent's career at Goupil's, he nevertheless carried forward with him the knowledge he had gained there – the thorough schooling in the trends, values and practices of the art market. Indeed, even after his dismissal his connection would continue, since his brother Theo ran the Montmartre branch of Goupil's, the very gallery where, by the mid-1880s, Theo would exhibit work of the Impressionists. Nevertheless, in 1876, the road for Vincent led elsewhere.

TEACHER AND CHRISTIAN EVANGELIST, APRIL 1876–SEPTEMBER 1880

Thirsty for success after being sacked from Goupil's, Vincent sought a fresh start in life by applying for a teaching position in England. This was a way of putting the past behind him and he relished the challenge of teaching French and German through a third language,

KEYWORD

Congregationalist: a type of independent Protestant church.

English. He dreamt of a life serving others and he was drawn to England as a beacon of culture. Soon after his twenty-third birthday in April 1876, he took unpaid work at a school in Ramsgate, Kent. In June, the school, and Vincent with it, moved to Isleworth in Middlesex and in July he found a paid position as a teacher in the same village. His new employer was a **Congregationalist** Minister, Thomas Slade-Jones, and when he gave Vincent the opportunity to preach the word of God in local chapels, he further whetted Vincent's appetite for full-time evangelism. This was a hunger that became a craving, with Vincent increasingly obsessed by religion.

His parents, however, were determined to restore their son to 'normality'. And so it was that in January 1877, thanks to some further string-pulling by his Uncle Cent, Van Gogh was found a job in a bookshop in Dordrecht, 30 km (18.5 miles) north of Etten, now the family home. But Vincent remained bound to religion, writing sermons and translating the Bible, even in office hours. Certain that he had been called by God, Vincent was a driven soul. No bookshop could cure him; the pull of the pulpit was far too strong.

With no less than the priesthood in mind, Vincent needed a theology degree and so, to secure a place at Amsterdam University, he began to study hard. Latin, Greek and Maths were vital qualifying subjects and, from May 1877 to July 1878, Vincent fought valiantly to master them, but even with professional help it proved a futile task. It was a sign of Vincent's persistence that he did not lose heart. As university proved too ambitious a goal, he decided to train to be an evangelist instead. This took him, at the age of 25, to a missionary college on the outskirts of Brussels. Vincent's tutors looked askance at their new pupil, seeing no future for him and, in fact, he remained there only three months. But Vincent was not daunted and their perception of him as an abject failure simply brought him closer to his ideal of selfless sacrifice.

As before, he simply changed tack. In December 1878, Vincent travelled south to Mons where, in a bleak enclave called the Borinage, 'the wretched of the earth' mined coal in a bitter battle for existence. Devoted but unpaid, Vincent intended to bring to them the love of God, through sermons and bible readings. Sadly, his efforts were little appreciated by the mining community. Nevertheless, for six months he was given some paid work by a missionary society as a lay preacher in the same village, Wasmes. However, because his piety was so extreme (he slept on straw like an animal and gave away his surplus clothes), his employers dismissed him.

Not to be defeated, in July 1879 Vincent simply moved 6 km (3.5 miles) east to Cuesmes. Here he remained until September 1880, working as an unpaid missionary and helper and also practising as an *artist*. In evocative drawings, Vincent recorded the back-breaking work of the miners – men, women and children – as in *Bearers of the Burden* (1881) now in the Kröller-Müller Museum, Netherlands. Vincent's choice of

KEYWORD

Lithographs: a design is drawn with greasy chalk on a flat stone which is then wetted. Because the printing ink is also greasy it will only print the greasy design and not the wet surrounding areas.

reading matter was particularly apt. It included the best 'teach yourself' drawing courses by Bargue and Gérôme (large-format **lithographs** of drawings of the human figure, graded for difficulty), as well as socially-conscious novels such as Charles Dickens's *Hard Times*.

TAKING UP PAINT: BELGIUM AND HOLLAND, OCTOBER 1880–FEBRUARY 1886

During the next period of his life, Vincent van Gogh became established as an artist. He began and ended this phase in Belgium (Brussels and Antwerp), but the largest part of the time (April 1881 to November 1885) was spent in his Dutch homeland. Hence it is known as Vincent's 'Dutch Period'. On the personal front, Vincent faced emotional crises, including three troubled liaisons: in 1881 with his cousin, the widow Kee Vos; in 1882–3 with a prostitute, Sien Hoornick (the subject of many of Vincent's best early works); and in 1884 with a next door neighbour, Margot Begemann. Although these led to terrible strains within the Van Gogh family, this was also the time when Vincent's brother Theo, an art dealer in Paris, began regular payments to Vincent in exchange for his pictures. Vincent saw this as a sort of contract and it gave him a degree of much-needed financial security.

Twice during this period Vincent stayed with his family and each time his art became bolder. First at Etten (April to November 1881) and then at Nuenen (December 1883 to November 1885), where his work most famously included a series of studies of peasants' heads, culminating in *The Potato Eaters* (1885), see Illustration 2, p. 38. As already mentioned, however, he began this stage of his career in

KEYWORDS

Impressionist: artists who rebelled against traditional art and recorded rural and urban scenes with a new spontaneity, a freshness of colour and sensitivity to the effects of light.

Brussels, where he pursued piecemeal art training until April 1881. Specifically, he continued with Bargue's teach yourself books, drew from live models and made contact with three Dutch artists in particular. The first, Willem Roelofs, was a precursor of the Dutch **Impressionists**. Roelofs advised Vincent to go to the Brussels Academy of Art (although it is known only that Vincent *applied* to join). He also urged Vincent to paint **en plein air**: Vincent certainly followed this advice and, in 1883, went to the wild environment of Drenthe in the north-east of the Netherlands, where Roelofs himself had painted. The second Dutch artist, Anthon van Rappard, had been a pupil of the French Academician, Baron

Gérôme. Vincent worked for a time in van Rappard's studio and went on sketching trips with him. The third artist, Adrien-Jean Madiol, gave Vincent more formal lessons.

These fragmented experiences contrast with the months of intensive study that Vincent spent in The Hague during early 1882 with his cousin by marriage, the landscapist Anton Mauve. This tuition built up Vincent's self-confidence and, during the next 12 months, he created atmospheric seascapes in oil paint and many powerful studies of 'people types'. These included fishermen and 'orphan men' from an old people's home run by the Dutch Reformed Church, as well as portraits of his girlfriend, Sien. They were executed in a variety of media – pencil, crayon, chalk, charcoal, watercolour and lithographic print. From this body of work, Vincent began to produce an ambitious portfolio of lithographs, 'Prints for the People', but he lacked sufficient funds to complete it.

The only occasion when we know for sure that Vincent studied at an art academy during this time was from January to February 1886, when he took lessons at the Antwerp Academy. Although Vincent had grave doubt about the academy itself, he produced some vigorous oil portraits (much freer in the handling of paint than his peasant heads at Nuenen), a superb study of a discus thrower and lively chalk sketches of dance halls.

Nevertheless, the dark side of this period in Vincent's life cannot be ignored. He fell out with his mentor Anton Mauve over his 'scandalous' liaison with the prostitute Sien, and he constantly clashed with his parents over his relationships with women.

Yet even if this was a time of conflict, it was also a time when Vincent's formidable potential was released. His horizons expanded and he himself taught still-life painting in Eindhoven. He received his first commissions from his Uncle Cor and, at the age of 32 in April 1885, he painted what has been called his first masterpiece, *The Potato Eaters*.

The foundation was now laid for Vincent's move to Paris, where his creative endeavours would reach new heights.

SEEING THE LIGHT: PARIS, MARCH 1886–FEBRUARY 1888

With the benefit of hindsight, we can see that when Vincent van Gogh reached Paris in March 1886, his artistic career had already passed the halfway mark. However, his creative powers had yet to reach their zenith.

As an art dealer in Paris in 1875–6, Vincent had felt alienated, but now in 1886, as an artist, Paris spelt liberation. He could experience art at the 'cutting edge': in May to June the Impressionists' last group exhibition; in August to September, the Independents' Salon. The young leaders of the **Pointillists**, Seurat and Signac, 'hung' at both these shows and

> **KEYWORD**
>
> Pointillists: artists who applied colour in dots, say a blue next to a yellow which, when viewed from a certain distance, should mix to form green ('optical mixture').

they, with Pissarro, the oldest of the Impressionists, would help to revolutionize Vincent's art and they also exhibited alongside him. That they inspired Vincent is shown by his scenes of the city, his views of Asnières and La Grande Jatte, and his portraits – of himself and of the art dealers 'Père' ('Father') Tanguy and Alexander Reid.

The art historian David Sweetman has suggested that Reid and Vincent's eventual falling out was because Reid and Theo van Gogh were rivals in the market for the paintings of Adolphe Monticelli. Vincent greatly admired Monticelli's flower paintings, and it was these images of blazing colour that inspired Vincent's first expressive forays into flower paintings in the summer of 1886.

Vincent's brother Theo was already supporting Vincent with money, but in Paris he also let Vincent lodge with him. First, in what is now Rue Victor-Massé, near Degas's studio and the Chat Noir cabaret, then from June 1886, at 54 Rue Lepic in Montmartre. Here Vincent also occupied a studio space – not far from his tutor Cormon's *atelier* (studio) where Vincent studied.   At times, Vincent proved an obnoxious flatmate, antagonizing people and leaving his room in a mess. Yet Theo, tolerant beyond the call of duty, took Vincent to exhibitions, classical music concerts and artists' studios, and went with him to the Chat Noir and Lapin Agile cabarets and the Nouvelle Athènes café, where the discussions that took place often sank into verbal warfare between (and within) the **modernist** factions.

> **KEYWORD**
>
> Modernist: the cutting-edge movements that made up the contemporary art scene.

By early 1888, Vincent could stand the arguing and polemics no more. He was also ill, suffering from over-indulgence in fatty meat, pipe tobacco, absinth, and adulterated wine quaffed beyond limit. He had bad teeth and he had contracted syphilis. In addition, two years of feverish work had stretched his nerves to breaking-point. The winter of 1887 was bitter and when, in February 1888, his friend Gauguin – whom he had first met at an exhibition in 1887 – decamped to Brittany, this must have added to Vincent's misery. Vincent's bright vision of Paris was fast becoming a nightmare. However, the bad experiences were themselves a blessing, for they triggered his pilgrimage to the South of France where, in Arles and St-Rémy, the glory of his genius would at last be revealed.

VISIONS OF THE SOUTH: ARLES AND ST-RÉMY, FEBRUARY 1888–MAY 1890

We have seen why Vincent wished to put Paris behind him. But what drew him to the South? His friend Toulouse-Lautrec had certainly sung its praises and Vincent craved the Mediterranean light that had inspired artists like Delacroix to paint so vividly.

Did the South of France also represent some sort of cultural ideal for Vincent? Certainly it may have brought him closer to the **aesthetics** of the Japanese art he so admired. Vivid natural forms, studied under the bright skies, could

KEYWORD

Aesthetics: relating to a sense of beauty.

perhaps help Vincent to reach the creative soul of the Japanese, 'who live in nature as if they themselves were flowers' (L542*). Japanese artists showed mutual respect by exchanging paintings and, as Vincent's friends Gauguin and Bernard – who themselves exchanged portraits with him – worked together in Brittany, so Vincent wished to build a creative community of like-minded artists in the South. Artists joining together in a collective was his ideal at this time.

The character of the Mediterranean landscape inspired Vincent deeply (see *Harvest at La Crau* (1888), Illustration 4, p. 43). So did the character of the few friends he made in Arles and the portraits that he made of them convey this strongly. These include Marie Ginoux, who ran the Café de la Gare (the *Night Café* (1888)) with her husband Joseph; a gardener, Patience Escalier; Eugène Boch, a Belgian artist; Lieut. Milliet, who had fought in French Indo-China (Vietnam) and to whom Vincent gave painting lessons; and the supportive Roulin family. Vincent found it hard to get others to model for him and so only one-fifth of his 170 Arles paintings are portraits. Nevertherless, they are among his greatest. In the Roulin family series of November 1888, Vincent used colour symbolically to contrast and connect parents and children. He had already moved beyond Impressionism.

For his first eight months in Arles, Vincent lived in hotels and cafés, but in September 1888 he was able to move into the 'Yellow House', celebrated in his famous paintings of his bedroom and in his view of the house sitting in its town square, a portrait in its own right. Although this period was to be highly productive, Vincent ate little but drank vast amounts of coffee to keep him 'keyed up' (L581).

In October 1888, Gauguin arrived from Paris – the genesis, Vincent hoped, of his ideal – an artists' commune, a 'Japan of the South'. But by December things were becoming fraught. Vincent's insecurity was fuelled when he heard that Theo had become engaged to be married. Meanwhile, the fruitful artistic collaboration with Gauguin was descending into furious argument. Vincent suffered his first mental seizures (a form of epilepsy) and savagely mutilated his ear with a razor. Between 24 December 1888 and 23 March 1889, he was in and out of the local psychiatric ward three times; an experience which, nevertheless, inspired one of his most brilliant compositions, *Dormitory of the Hospital* (April 1889).

Craving better health and a chance to paint in peace, in May 1889 Vincent became a voluntary patient in an asylum near St-Rémy. Here, at the age of 36, he was to create some of his greatest works, notably *The Starry Night* (1889). Yet, although Vincent made a slow reconnection with the outside world, it was not to last. In June 1889, his doctors first allowed him to paint – supervized – outdoors. But in July, following a return visit to Arles, he had a fearsome seizure and in the process ate some toxic paint. Now he had to spend the next three months inside the asylum. But defeat was far from Vincent's mind and he never gave up on his painting. Not only was this the time of his quintessential self-portrait of September 1889, but he was also executing oil paintings based on engravings of the classic works of Rembrandt, Delacroix and Millet.

By December 1889, Vincent was able to send three parcels of new paintings to Theo in Paris. In January 1890 he had an enthusiastic review from a young critic, Albert Aurier. In February, further successes came when his canvas *The Red Vineyard* (1888) fetched 400 francs at an exhibition in Brussels. In March, ten of Vincent's pictures were hung at the Independents' show in Paris, where they were highly praised by Monet. Thus, Vincent could celebrate his thirty-seventh birthday on 30 March, knowing that he was rising out of obscurity. Unfortunately his seizures continued. Two came in December 1889 and in January 1890 one lasted a whole week and he suffered another heavy attack in February after he visited Marie Ginoux, his former landlady in Arles. This one continued until the end of April 1890.

THE PILGRIM RETURNS: AUVERS, MAY–JULY 1890

Where could Vincent find new strength and who might help him? Already by October 1889 he had thought of turning north again. Finally, in May 1890, he made the break, with the aim of going to Auvers, where he had heard from Theo that the homoeopathic doctor, Paul Gachet, lived. There were also artistic motives. Paris, in 1888, had seen him yearning for the South; now, he saw in the north a new country, ripe for his imagination.

En route to the north, Vincent spent a few days in Theo and his wife Johanna's new flat in a secluded Paris apartment block called the Cité Pigalle. In this Aladdin's cave, filled with Vincent's paintings, he and his brother pored over the stacks of masterpieces that had yet to find a buyer. Despite his traumas, Vincent seemed to radiate good health and happiness.

His ultimate destination of Auvers lay at some distance from the capital. That Cézanne had painted *The Suicide's House* (1873) there seems prophetic now. However, Auvers also had close connections with Vincent's friend Pissarro and Pissarro, too, knew Dr Gachet. Gachet had, so Theo and Pissarro thought, the skills needed to save Vincent from his tortured self.

When Vincent reached Auvers, he did find a security of sorts, staying at a friendly inn and talking art at Gachet's house on the outskirts of town. He continued to experiment and from this final period of Vincent's creative life comes his only etching – of Gachet smoking a pipe. Vincent was also using a new panoramic format, the 'double square', in which he painted a series of eight magnificently brooding landscapes, most famously *Wheatfield with Crows* (July 1890).

In the early summer of 1890, Vincent was producing, on average, one painting each day. Nevertheless his moods swung painfully from elation to dejection; the highs were too brief to relieve the lows. Vincent hated being dependent on others, not least on his loyal brother Theo and his would-be healer, Dr Gachet.

With the last letter that he posted to Theo, dated 24 July 1890, Vincent enclosed sketches for new paintings and asked for art supplies. Yet he also talked pessimistically of painters being on the defensive, and of personal initiative being futile. In the end, the burden of life and loneliness and his sense of being a burden on others became too great. Behind the château of Auvers, close to where he had recently been painting, Vincent shot himself. He died two days later, on 29 July, in the arms of his brother.

Among the many who were present at Vincent's funeral on the following day, were two close friends from his Paris days, 'Père' Tanguy and Emile Bernard. There were other echoes of the past, for it was the twenty-first anniversary of Vincent starting work at Goupil's in The Hague. In death, Vincent had come of age.

* * *SUMMARY* * *

- Vincent came from a religious background. Although he rebelled against family constraints, he would later return to religion as a refuge from unhappiness.

- His education was erratic, but it nurtured his love of art, languages and literature.

- Although Vincent's career as an art dealer ended in dismissal, art remained important to him and in 1880 he decided to become a professional artist.

- Vincent's brother Theo sent him money in exchange for paintings, which he attempted to sell. The many letters that Vincent wrote to Theo are an important resource for the literature of art.

- In Paris (1886–88) Vincent befriended modern artists such as Bernard, Gauguin and Signac. His technique and use of colour became more dynamic.

- The South of France (1888-90) further liberated Vincent's art. His paintings of its changing seasons, its townscapes and some of its characterful inhabitants are among his greatest works.

- However, Vincent's health began to suffer badly, and for a year he consigned himself to an asylum. Despite his health problems, Vincent's artistic imagination was not impaired.

- Vincent's personal equilibrium and ease with the world were precarious. He committed suicide at the age of 37.

Forces at Work – Influences on Van Gogh's Art and Mind

AN EXTENDED FAMILY: THE VAN GOGH CLAN

As we have already seen, Vincent's family was linked to him by more than blood ties. Through a number of close relationships – parents, siblings, uncles and aunts, cousins – there existed connections with Vincent's changing world. On the positive side, there was financial support and professional advice and inspiration, but on the more negative side, there were emotional ties that could prove destructive, leading, on occasion, to dismay, bitterness and conflict. Not least, between Vincent and his father love turned cold and though relations later improved, it was no eccentric whim that led Van Gogh to sign his name Vincent, without the surname. Part of the reason was that foreigners found it hard to pronounce Van Gogh, but it is of greater psychological significance that he wrote to Theo in December 1883, 'Essentially I am *not* a "Van Gogh".' (L345a). Despite this protestation, it was Theo van Gogh, his brother and brother-in-art, who financed his painting and funded his recuperative stay in the St-Rémy asylum – the retreat which was to yield some of Vincent's most profoundly original works.

For Vincent's life in art, his extended family proved highly significant. It was thanks to Uncle Cent that he took up an apprenticeship with Goupil's, dealers in fine art and Uncle Cor arranged commissions for his work. Through the marriage of Aunt Fie's daughter Jet to Anton Mauve, Vincent met the artist who would nurture his talent in The Hague. Conversely, when his cousin Kee, Uncle Stricker's daughter, rebuffed him, he turned in his dejection to Sien Hoornick, the prostitute who also became his model. This volatile relationship sparked a chain of events that would take Vincent to Nuenen (December 1883 to November 1885), launching a key phase in his artistic development.

IN THE BEGINNING WAS THE WORD: RELIGION

Although in 1881 his uncle, the Reverend J.P. Stricker, conspired to sabotage Vincent's last attempt to win his daughter's love, he had not always been Vincent's foe. Indeed, only four years earlier Uncle Stricker had been venerated by Vincent as a leading authority on Jesus. And the religious circles in which Stricker moved in Amsterdam were famous for their great Christian preachers, notably Eliza Laurillard and Jan Jacob ten Kate. These preachers were influential on Van Gogh and the themes they chose for their sermons, taken from nature and from rural life, would help to define the imagery of his art: sowers, reapers, sunflowers and the sun itself. They spoke of nature's eternal cycle of birth, death and rebirth, echoed by the human activities that accompany it year on year – sowing, cultivation and harvest. A close look at the fecund landscape of Vincent's *Sower with Setting Sun* (1888), after Millet, where the sower is at one with the earth which he sows, reveals the primary value that Vincent himself attached to such life-giving tasks.

What of the 'fruits of the earth' themselves? For Vincent, an often-repeated symbol or 'emblem' of worship was the sunflower, as it turned devotedly towards the sun. The sun itself could represent the loved one, nature, the artist-hero (for example, Monticelli), God or Christ. The

KEYWORDS

Oeuvre: body of work as a whole.

Subliminal: subconscious.

thread of religious imagery that runs through Vincent's art has been explored by the Japanese Van Gogh scholar, Tsukasa Kōdera. Kōdera concludes that an analysis of the thematic structure of Vincent's **oeuvre** and the frequency with which he used certain 'emblems', shows how he expressed deeply-held Christian feelings through images from nature.

READING MAKETH A FULL MAN: LITERATURE

In Vincent's paintings, religious references were normally oblique or **subliminal**. However, the subject matter of *Still Life with Bible* (1885) shows him confronting the issue of religion directly. A large, open family Bible (the 'old gospel' of the past) lies on a table juxtaposed with Emile Zola's novel *La Joie de Vivre*, a 'new gospel' of Naturalist literature and the sort of serious writing that would speak truth to the modern generation. The Bible and the Zola novel in this picture have also been interpreted as representing the conflict between Vincent's father's traditional world and his own modern one.

Such paintings were described as 'manifesto pictures' by Druick and Zegers (see Further Reading section) in that they tell us of Vincent's values and expectations. Another work of this kind is Vincent's still life *Romans Parisiens* (Parisian Novels, 1887), which depicts a whole group of books, a collection, just as Vincent, in his own creative output, wished his paintings to be seen as a body of work. A beautifully judged composition, *Drawing Board, Pipe, Onions and Sealing Wax*, painted in January 1889, less than a month after the 'ear' incident, portrays a letter from Theo and a popular health manual by the hygienist François Vincent Raspail. It was Raspail who recommended the use of camphor (though as an antidote to parasites), a substance that Vincent inhaled to help him sleep.

Vincent inhabited a 'bookish' society that treasured the classics of literature, yet kept abreast of modern trends. Vincent himself believed that literature made one more spiritual and that it enhanced 'being'. For friends and relatives he copied out his favourite poems to inspire them.

Some of Vincent's earliest readings were **devotional texts**, including *Imitation of Christ* (1418) by the German monk Thomas à Kempis. This book, rediscovered by Vincent's father's generation, taught the reader to emulate Jesus through humility and service.

> **KEYWORD**
>
> Devotional texts: texts concerned with religious faith.

While John Bunyan's *Pilgrim's Progress* (1678) nourished Vincent's belief in life as a spiritual journey, *Life of Jesus* (1863) by Joseph-Ernest Renan explored Christ's humanity and his moral teachings.

Vincent was deeply interested in history too; it stimulated his imagination. When for a time he turned fanatically to God in the later 1870s, he instinctively moved away from the writings of France's national historian Jean Michelet,

KEYWORD

Plasticity: three-dimension-ality, i.e. 'realness'.

because of the latter's anti-clericalism. Ultimately, however, he could not resist Michelet's inspiring history of the French Revolution (1789) and soon readmitted it as a source of intellectual nourishment. Moreover, like Bunyan, Michelet was a 'champion of the people'. Vincent's sense of history came partly from the English historian Thomas Carlyle, who venerated heroic figures who had revived the soul of humankind, such as Christ and Mohammed. The same could be said of those whom Vincent saw as leaders of the arts, such as Shakespeare and Zola. Zola, whose novels Vincent discovered in The Hague (and whose *La Joie de Vivre* he depicted), was leader of the French 'Naturalists'. The Naturalist authors captured contemporary life in the raw, with an honest view of people and society that Vincent respected. For Vincent, Zola 'painted with words', so tangible was the reality he portrayed; Vincent had equal admiration for the English novelists Charlotte Brontë, George Eliot and Charles Dickens. He praised them for their **plasticity** and their 'awakening power' (R43).

At the end of *Notes from a Literary Life* by Fieke Pabst and Evert van Uitert, the list of literary sources with which Vincent was familiar – poetry and prose, religious and secular – takes up over nine large-format pages, each with four columns. Pabst and van Uitert cite one of Vincent's pupils in Nuenen who described Vincent as a 'colossal man of letters'. This heroic literary record both paralleled and helped to shape Vincent's towering achievement in art. Fascinating evidence of Vincent's love of literature is found in the books he portrayed in his paintings, such as in *Still Life with Bible* (1885) and *Portrait of Dr. Gachet* (1890).

ART THAT INSPIRED

In his creative vision, Vincent was influenced by certain artists and movements in particular. He admired the richly expressive Dutch masters such as Rembrandt and Frans Hals; the Romantic painters – notably Delacroix – with their highly charged use of colour; the compositionally daring Japanese printmakers, whose prints Vincent collected so avidly; and the innovative work of his contemporaries in Paris during the period 1886–8.

Three other direct sources of inspiration, described more fully below, were the English 'Black and White' illustrators, Jean-François Millet (1814–75), and Adolphe Monticelli (1824–86).

The 'Black and Whites'

Vincent wrote to his friend Rappard in February 1883 about the work of British artists and illustrators such as Hubert Herkomer (1849–1914), Frank Holl (1845–88) and Luke Fildes (1844–1927), 'There is something stimulating and invigorating like old wine about those striking, powerful, virile drawings.' (R23). Indeed, in many of his 59 letters to Rappard, Vincent discussed at length these 'Black and White' illustrators, so called after their dramatic monochrome drawings. Commissioned by *The Graphic* and *The Illustrated London News*, their significance was both artistic and social. With fine and sensitive draughtsmanship, often translated through the disciplined medium of **wood-engraving**, these illustrators treated themes of social concern, such as the plight of the poor, the homeless and the sick.

KEYWORD

Wood-engraving: the wood-engraver takes a block of wood cut across the grain, and, using a sharp tool, makes the design by cutting away the non-printing areas to create a relief block. Wood-engraving was frequently used in the nineteenth century for illustrated books and magazines.

The 'Black and Whites' were inspiring to Vincent in their pictorial power and in their compassionate understanding of suffering humanity. He found their subject matter highly relevant too and he was drawn to their images of political turmoil, such as the revolutionary Paris Commune of 1871, and to scenes of social deprivation, notably homelessness and hunger. Not only did Vincent's favourite 'Black and Whites' include celebrated illustrators like Holl and Fildes, but other figures such as Caton Woodville (1856–1927), who drew the series *The State of Ireland* for *The Illustrated London News* in 1880, which focused on rural poverty in Galway and Connemara. Vincent also found that some of their compositions spoke to him in a more personal way, with subject matter familiar to him from his time in England. For example, *Clapham Road* by Gordon Thompson was a view with which Vincent was familiar from the days when he lived in north Brixton, and it took him on a voyage of rediscovery.

The 'Black and Whites', whose prints Vincent bought with Theo's help in The Hague, triggered off other associations for him, for example with Albrecht Dürer (1471–1528). Realism, originality, sincerity and the use of bold contour were the strengths that linked the prints of this Renaissance artist to those of the 'Black and Whites'. In a more practical way, Vincent was attracted to the latter's chosen drawing medium, printer's ink, through which he found a new way to produce dramatic work with pen and brush.

Vincent's admiration for the 'Black and Whites', reflecting as they did his own concern for social issues and his belief that art should confront truths about the world and express a deep humanity, was to continue throughout his career.

Jean-François Millet (1814–75)

'Millet is someone I will not argue about, although I do not refuse to discuss him.'

Vincent to Rappard, June 1885

(R52*)

'Millet is the voice of wheat.'

Vincent to Isaäcson, a Dutch painter and critic, May 1890

(L614a*)

Millet, the son of a peasant, lived in rural Normandy until the age of 24, then moved to Paris where he exhibited his paintings at the Salon. Millet's canvases portray peasants larger than life and with an earthy yet spiritual quality (notably in *The Angelus*, 1858–9) that registered strongly in Van Gogh's imagination. In contrast to Van Gogh, Millet was neither a

KEYWORDS

Canon: the recognized work of an artist.

Heliographic: pictures created by early photography.

vivid colourist nor a *plein air* painter. However, his themes – sowers, diggers, the harvest – would frequently recur in Vincent's **canon** of work.

Vincent also identified with Millet's sayings, for example with his statement, quoted by Sensier (see below), that 'I would never do away with suffering, for it is often what makes artists express themselves more forcefully.' When writing about the 'essentials' for building up a serious body of work, Vincent quoted Millet's remark that, in order to do so, one needed to 'work like several slaves' (to Theo, July 1885, L418). As a painter, Vincent's habit of driving himself to the limits of exhaustion is well known.

It was Alfred Sensier's beautifully bound and uplifting biography of Millet (1881), with its **heliographic** reproductions of Millet's paintings, that fuelled Vincent's determination to paint scenes of peasant life, such as *The Potato Eaters* (1885). Though one would not call *The Potato Eaters* comforting, comfort is exactly what Vincent found in Millet's own paintings. 'One asks oneself if he made them like that expressly in order to comfort us' (To Wil, his sister, January 1890, W19).

In the last year of his life, Vincent found consolation in improvizing colour on copies he made of engravings 'after Millet'. 'And then my brush goes between my fingers as a bow would on the violin, and absolutely for my own pleasure' (To Theo, September 1889, L607). The wish that others might discover a similar pleasure was also close to

Vincent's heart; he believed that children would be inspired to become painters if they could only see reproductions of Millet's work in their schools.

Adolphe Monticelli (1824–86)

'… a little cracked, or rather very much so … of an extremely refined taste as a colourist, a thoroughbred man of a rare race, continuing the best traditions of the past.'

Vincent to his sister Willemina, Autumn 1888

(W8)

As a young artist, Monticelli attended two Ecoles des Beaux Arts, the first in Marseilles (his birthplace), the second in Paris. Here, like Vincent 30 years later, he visited the Louvre and was inspired by the paintings of Delacroix. Following his father's death, Monticelli spent six months in a monastery, while continuing to paint. Coincidentally, the St-Rémy asylum where Vincent stayed and painted had also been a monastery. At the end of his life, Monticelli was completely paralysed, except for the use of his eyes. He died, aged 64, in the very year that Vincent arrived in Paris and first encountered Monticelli's vibrant flower paintings, among them the *Vase with Flowers*, now in the Van Gogh Museum in Amsterdam.

One reading of Vincent's *Sunflowers* (1888/89) is that they are an allusion to Monticelli and his 'Provençale' palette of yellow, 'sulphur' and orange. The surface textures of *Sunflowers*, as in Monticelli's later works, are applied sculpturally, with an expressive **impasto**. As well as being inspired by Monticelli's flower studies, Vincent also found inspiration in his intense evocations of the sun rising and setting over the southern landscape. 'To whom I owe so much' (L626a), is how Vincent described

KEYWORD

Impasto: raised texture resulting from thick application of paint.

Monticelli in a letter to the critic Albert Aurier (February 1890). In late 1888, Vincent even thought he might go on a pilgrimage to Marseilles, dressed like Monticelli from head to foot.

For Vincent, a powerful sense of colour and commanding draughtsmanship connected Monticelli to the French 'Romantic' painter Delacroix. When he was in Paris and the South of France, Vincent saw himself following in Monticelli's footsteps like a son or brother. He sought to 'resurrect' Monticelli by incorporating his masterly range of tones and colours into his own work. But these triumphant attempts were not won without a struggle. Vincent suffered the same nervous strain he believed Monticelli had endured as, in the searing heat of summer, he orchestrated on his canvas the counterpoint and harmony of colours. Vincent felt he also understood deeply the pain and anguish of Monticelli's last years, which he compared to Gethsemane, the scene of Christ's agony before his crucifixion.

INNER FORCES: HEALTH AND SELF

There have been hundreds of attempts to dissect Vincent's health problems and the online forum (www.vangoghgallery.com) shows that debate on the subject continues to flourish. Discussions have included various theories, a few of which are described below, with some viewpoints noted alongside.

Psychological

* Attention Deficit Hyperactive Disorder: One symptom is hypersensitivity, which could lead one to 'feel' colours, 'see' sound, etc.

* Bipolar (manic) depression: Vincent's highs were 'goal orientated' and he harnessed them in bursts of creativity.

* Schizophrenia: The associated chemical adrenochrome could help explain Vincent's use of very bright colours.

Physical

* Untreated venereal disease: Leading to neurological problems and physical debility.

* Porphyria: Of the acute-intermittent variety, leading to gastric complaints, hypertension and psychosis.

* Tinnitus: In extreme cases, this could lead to hallucinations.

Self-Inflicted

* Drugs: Did Vincent take a herbal remedy that made him see yellow haloes around certain objects?

* Lead poisoning: From paint inhalation and licking his brushes. Hence Vincent's dizziness and need for the open air.

Beyond these theories, a good deal of scholarly attention has been paid to Menière's Syndrome (for example, in the *Journal of the American Medical Association*) and temporal lobe epilepsy (in a paper submitted to the 1990 Van Gogh centenary symposium and in the *Journal of the History of Neuroscience*). The author of these last two articles, the Dutch psychologist P.H.A. Voskuil, concluded that Van Gogh had an abnormality in the left temporal lobe of the brain and that this, combined with other factors such as neurosis, and exacerbated by indulgence in absinth, could have led Vincent to what the neurologist Sir W.R. Gowers called in 1907, the 'border-land' of epilepsy. It could also have contributed to Vincent's suicide. Voskuil himself concluded his *Journal of the History of Neuroscience* article: 'It was not because of the disease but in spite of it, and based on strength of character, creativity, sensitivity and high intelligence, that Van Gogh painted his wonderful paintings' ('Vincent van Gogh's malady – a test case for the relationship between temporal lobe dysfunction and epilepsy?', 1992, p.161).

What is certain is that Vincent's will to creative self-expression transcended any debilitating illnesses he may have suffered. Beyond any moral, spiritual and financial motives, this was his life-giving force. It sprang from everything he saw, sensed and experienced – from the people he encountered, the culture he absorbed and the land he travelled through. Long walks, for example, allowed Vincent to commune with nature, to contemplate his inner self and to connect what he saw with images from art and literature; he enjoyed sleeping out under the stars and waking very early, on one occasion hiking 160 km (100 miles) from Ramsgate in Kent to Welwyn in Hertfordshire, to see his sister Anna who was a teacher there.

'At half past three in the morning the birds began to sing at sight of dawn and I set off again. It was fine to walk then.'

Vincent to Theo, June 1876
(L69)

* * *SUMMARY* * *

• Vincent's family provided him with many opportunities, but sometimes they were offended by his behaviour and, equally, he sometimes felt constricted by their expectations.

• Although Vincent became disillusioned with the Church, symbols of worship and the cycle of life continued to feature in his art.

• Vincent had an enormous appetite for literature and was inspired by a wide range of authors, both religious and secular.

• Vincent 'knew his art'. Of the many artists he admired, two that he found particularly inspiring were Jean-François Millet and Adolphe Monticelli. He also admired the social content of the English 'Black and White' artists.

• There is something of an 'industry' where theories about Vincent's ill-health are concerned. It is likely that a complex of factors was involved and that a form of epilepsy was the most significant.

3 Vincent – the English Connection

INTRODUCTION

It is widely acknowledged that Vincent's years in Paris (March 1886 to February 1888) inspired him to use the full spectrum of colour in his painting. It is, perhaps, less well known that the periods he spent in London were equally formative for his art, for the subjects he chose to draw and paint and for the concepts that lay behind them.

From 1873 to 1876 Vincent van Gogh spent the major part of his time in England, working, except for three months in Kent, in and around London. As the art historian Martin Bailey affirms, Vincent was the only **Post-Impressionist** immersed in English culture. Yet, far from turning him into an Englishman, his English experiences helped him to *transcend* nationality. As Vincent wrote to Carolien Haanebeek in February 1874, 'At

times I am inclined to believe that I am practically turning into a cosmopolite; that is, neither a Dutchman, nor an Englishman, nor yet a Frenchman but simply a *man*' (L13a).

ART WORLDS: VINCENT AS SALESMAN, OBSERVER AND DRAUGHTSMAN

Salesman

As we have already seen, Vincent was promoted from The Hague to Goupil's London branch in May 1873 and he arrived in England aged 20. The intoxicating vitality of London stood in marked contrast to the more sedate spirit of The Hague; while the rolling hills and parks of Surrey, where Vincent liked to walk, could not have been more different from the flat landscapes and endless horizons of rural Holland.

Vincent walked 3 km (2 miles) to work every morning. Goupil's, in Southampton Street off the Strand, lay close to the bustle of Covent Garden. It was an important branch of the London art scene and although not yet a gallery, was a busy wholesale dealer, where print sellers bought their stocks of high-quality reproductions. For almost a year things went very well at Goupil's and Vincent was part of a busy sales team, working hard and receiving a salary increase in January 1874. In his spare time he took up sketching on the Embankment and visited galleries, including the National Gallery and the recently-opened Bethnal Green Museum, where he was shocked by the surrounding East End slums.

By the time Vincent had returned to Goupil's, London, in early 1875 after his brief transfer to the Paris branch, the firm had moved up in the world and was repositioning itself as a high-profile gallery. Vincent now found himself selling paintings by the Barbizon and Hague Schools. However, this period was not to last, as once again Vincent was recalled to Paris (May 1875).

Observer

Writing to Theo in January 1874, Vincent listed 62 ('a few', L13) of the artists he most admired. Most were Dutch or French; only three were English. However, one of these, George Henry Boughton, was to hold a prominent place in Vincent's personal gallery of the 'greats'. Boughton's work, of which Vincent made some sketches, was handled by Goupil's and he favoured historical and literary themes. His painting *God Speed! Pilgrims Setting out for Canterbury; Time of Chaucer* helped to inspire Vincent's first sermon (see Preaching the Word section). Moreover, Vincent's list of heroes is deceptive, for the longer he stayed in England, the broader his outlook on English art became. London's galleries fed Vincent's appetite for 'art with a message', and in the Royal Academy's Summer Exhibitions he discovered the Social Realists. These socially concerned artists and illustrators recorded the 'Condition of England' question, the dark side of life described in Disraeli's *Sybil; or The Two Nations* (1845), and they had a major influence on Vincent's work in the 1880s. This can be seen in his portraits of the poor and homeless, in compositions of huddled groups, or in telling details which he pulled out of their original context and made his own. The Social Realists did not, however, dominate his perspective. Vincent visited art collections in and around London, such as Hampton Court and the Dulwich Picture Gallery; he became an admirer of the inspirational landscapes of Constable, Millais and Turner; and at the same time he retained his loyalty to the older European masters, such as Rembrandt and Frans Hals.

Draughtsman

The available evidence may not be a reliable guide to the extent of Vincent's artistic output in England. He may have drawn many more sketches than are now extant. Nevertheless, he completed several views taken from the Thames Embankment and, as well as these, 15 additional drawings are known from this time. Four of these relate to the house where he lodged in Hackford Road, Brixton; three are of churches; and three are views of Ramsgate (where he taught, April–June 1876). There are two copies of oil paintings by Boughton and Corot and three other drawings: one of houses in Isleworth in Middlesex (where he taught after Ramsgate), one of Streatham Common and one (subject unknown) for his Bible teacher in The Hague. Sadly, seven of these 15 pictures and all of the Thames Embankment views are lost – known to us only through references in family correspondence. The remaining drawings (the three churches, the houses in Isleworth, two of the Ramsgate drawings, the Corot copy and a view of Hackford Road) survive in the archives of the Van Gogh Museum in Amsterdam. In 1992, five of these were lent to the *Van Gogh in England* exhibition at the Barbican Art Gallery in London. The subjects of all these sketches must have had significance for Vincent.

Vincent's best surviving England sketches are a drawing of the Isleworth houses (July 1876) and an ink study of the Austin Friars

(Dutch Reformed) Church in London (November 1876). The former is deft in its use of texture and tone and the latter shows a fine command of line. Given this group of work, mainly of topographical English views and the visual training that Vincent undoubtedly received at the London branch of Goupil's, England could claim a significant role in Vincent's development as an artist.

UNREQUITED LOVE?

In August 1873, during his employment at Goupil's, Vincent moved to his second set of lodgings, at 87 Hackford Road, Brixton. The house was owned by Ursula Loyer, a widow who lived there with her daughter, Eugenie. There is one theory that Vincent fell in love with Eugenie but was rejected by her, and another theory that it was Ursula in whom he was interested. The art historian Martin Bailey conjectured in *Young Vincent: The Story of Van Gogh's Years in England* (1990) that Vincent may have felt deeply for both Eugenie and her mother. The first published account of Vincent's romantic attachment at that time came from his sister-in-law, Johanna van Gogh-Bonger, in her 'Memoir of Vincent van Gogh' (December 1913), an introductory essay to the first edition of the Letters (1914–15). However, she confused matters by incorrectly referring to the daughter as Ursula. She related that Vincent 'apparently spoke to Ursula of his love. Alas, it turned out that she was already engaged to the man who boarded with them before Vincent came. He tried everything to make her break this engagement, but he did not succeed.' If Eugenie was indeed the object of Vincent's desire, her unyielding commitment to her fiancé – Samuel Plowman, an amateur artist – must have been a painful blow. A third theory, according to research in the mid-1990s by the Dutch art historian, Elly Cassee, is that during this period Vincent was in love with his second cousin Carolien Haanebeek (and that Vincent's brother Theo was in love with Carolien's sister Annet).

Whatever the truth of any emotional relationship and the unhappiness that it may have caused, in 1874 Vincent did move away from Hackford

Road – but only 1.5 km (1 mile) away. Meanwhile, professional relationships at Goupil's were also becoming strained and in May 1875 he was transferred for the second time, permanently, to their Paris branch.

Art, already a source of strength and inspiration for Vincent in England, now became a consoling passion. His liking for English art and culture was not forgotten in this new beginning in the French capital. Settled in Montmartre, Vincent kept on his wall a print of a landscape by Richard Bonington (also a Montmartre resident, in the 1820s). Here in Montmartre, Vincent met Harry Gladwell, the heir to a prestigious art gallery in the City of London. Gladwell worked with Vincent in Goupil's and they became friends, discussing literature and reading the gospels together. Religion, like art, was ever more a fortifying source and consolation for Vincent. In time, he himself would preach; but first came the urge to teach.

TEACHING LANGUAGES
About education and educators, Van Gogh had mixed feelings. He had spent part of his childhood at schools that seemed distant from his home (1864–8) and in Amsterdam in 1878 he gave up on Latin and Greek, subjects he was studying in preparation for the priesthood. Then in Brussels, he failed a preliminary missionary course. Vincent fell out with his artist cousin and tutor Anton Mauve in 1882 and hated the teaching system at the Antwerp Art Academy (January to February 1886). Yet, his early schooling in the Netherlands had blessed him with some first-rate art tuition; he had learnt much about the painting profession in The Hague, London and Paris and he had a passion for English literature, especially admiring Charles Dickens and George Eliot. In addition, Vincent was a resolute self-improver. In 1876, it was two headmasters, William Stokes (a former artist) and Reverend T. Slade-Jones, who gave Vincent the chance of a new lease of life after the trauma of unrequited love and the collapse of his career with Goupil's. As with other stages in Vincent's life, however, nothing was to be straightforward.

Following Vincent's dismissal from Goupil's, various possibilities had been mooted, even that he should become a fully-fledged artist. But Vincent's **altruism** led him to seek fulfilment in teaching instead. He applied for

KEYWORD

Altruism: belief in living for the needs of others.

some posts and, just past his twenty-third birthday, after being away from England for nearly a year, he heard that he was to be taken on as an assistant master in Ramsgate, Kent. Private schools fulfilled a crucial role at a time when state primary education was at its infancy and, moreover, he would be following in the footsteps of his sister Anna who was teaching French and Music in Hertfordshire. A probationary position, with no pay but free board and lodging, were poor terms for a job, but it was a start and, furthermore, Vincent found Ramsgate's stormy coastline inspirational. His employer, the bald, be-whiskered William Stokes has been described (by Wilhelm Uhde, author of *Vincent van Gogh*, London, 1936) as 'a grotesque pedant, who had about twenty pale and underfed boarders in his house.' The inside of the school was dingily Dickensian, with rotten floorboards, bugs and broken windows. However, the Van Gogh scholar, Jan Hulsker, has more recently shown that, whatever the conditions, Vincent did in fact enjoy his teaching work there. He taught Mathematics, French and German, but found it difficult to make his lessons sink in. Nevertheless, he forged ahead, often dictating passages out loud. Yet Vincent was being taken advantage of. Although headmaster Stokes had earlier raised Vincent's hopes of a salary, when the school moved to Isleworth, Vincent's position remained unpaid.

Again, Vincent was at a crossroads. Where did the future lie now? A life in the New World? A return to the Netherlands? Or, closer to his present Isleworth home, working as a missionary in London? As fate would have it, he did not even have to travel that far, for in the same Isleworth street as Stoke's school there was another, run by a kindly – and salary-paying – headmaster, the Congregationalist, Reverend T. Slade-Jones.

Here, at Holme Court School, Vincent would teach every weekday morning, look after the Jones's children and teach them German (which he had already taught at Mr Stokes's school) in the afternoon, and in the evening put the boarders to bed and read them stories. The rest of his evening was free to write to his family, copy from the books he loved and study the New Testament.

PREACHING THE WORD: INNER STRENGTH FROM RELIGION

By the summer of 1876, Vincent was thinking seriously about entering the Church and on at least two occasions, 13 June and 23 September, visited a missionary in Kennington in South London. On the first occasion he took a letter with him, in which he described himself in ideal terms as well travelled, able to mix with all sorts of people, proficient in four languages, and having an 'innate love of the Church and everything connected with it' (enclosed with L69, 17 June 1876). On his second visit, a priest at the mission suggested that he might work at Liverpool docks, where his pastoral talents could be exercised to the full.

However, before any move to the north could occur, Vincent found fortune nearer home. This came about as a result of Reverend T. Slade-Jones's religious work, officiating in several nonconformist Churches south of the river Thames. He offered Vincent the opportunity to assist him in this work and so here Vincent took up his new vocation. He became increasingly active in Slade-Jones's Congregationalist Tabernacle in Turnham Green, contributing to its Sunday School teachers group, officiating at children's services on Thursday evenings and visiting their homes for bible study. An ecumenical Christian, Vincent recognized the spirit of the gospel in all denominations, not only Congregationalist but also Catholic, Anglican, Baptist and Methodist. He began speaking at prayer meetings at the Kew Road Methodist Church, Richmond, and in October 1876, thanks to Reverend T. Slade-Jones's influence, it was here that he preached his first sermon. In it he drew on his poetic interpretation of Boughton's painting of the Canterbury Pilgrims, to illustrate his message about man's progress through life: In humankind's search for God, life was a pilgrimage from Earth to Heaven. When love of Christ lay dormant, God himself could revive it and (expanding on the theme) man would experience doubts, but God could allay them. Sadness made one a better person because one could understand the sorrow of others; one should have the courage not to fear death at the end of life's journey.

More sermons followed in November 1876, for example at Petersham Methodist Chapel near Richmond Park. Here, Vincent expressed a wise faith in God and Man: God never disappeared from life for ever; behind failure there were blessings in disguise; in age lay maturity.

Vincent himself was now 23 and, though not old in years, he had been subject to a number of ageing experiences which had impressed themselves deeply on his intense nature. His life was now to take another new direction, as he moved back to the Netherlands in December 1876, but he had been enriched by the time he had spent in England and strong links with that country would remain throughout his life.

ENGLISH POSTSCRIPTS
A number of interesting examples are known of Vincent's continuing connection with British art and culture and, on a more personal level, with the friends he had made there:

Amsterdam
Vincent worshipped at the English Reformed Church in the Begijnhof (one of the oldest parts of Amsterdam), which drew its congregation largely from English-speaking people. He also taught at an Amsterdam Sunday School run by an English priest.

When Vincent was struggling with his studies for the priesthood in 1877, he received a heart-warming, one-off visit from his English art dealer friend and brother-in-faith, Harry Gladwell. Vincent had previously read the Bible with Gladwell in Paris and had been welcomed into his home.

Slade-Jones, Vincent's friend and employer from Isleworth, visited Vincent's family home in Etten and, through his missionary connections, helped to get Vincent onto a probationary course in mid-1878. Together, they also contemplated a joint scheme to build churches in the Borinage.

Brussels and The Hague

It was in Brussels and The Hague (1880–3) that the influence of the English 'Black and White' artists on Vincent's work reached its zenith. Their inspiration can be seen in Vincent's *Bearers of the Burden* (1881), in a pencil and ink drawing he made of miners' wives, weighed down by the crushing weight of coal and in *Sorrow* (1882), the pitiful and bleakly observed nude portrait of his girlfriend Sien.

Of those that survive, all of Van Gogh's titled watercolours and drawings, from May 1881 to November 1882, have English names. Vincent had thought of getting a job as an illustrator for *The Graphic* in London, and he believed that giving his pictures English names would attract English publishers. He contemplated returning to England in 1883, hurt by the withdrawal of Sien who was now preoccupied with her new-born baby (not fathered by Vincent). Vincent felt marginalized and he broke up with Sien. But would he actually opt for a return to England? Could he face the risk of yet more rejection? The lure of English culture notwithstanding, Vincent 'played safe' and spent another creative three years in the Netherlands.

The thought of returning to London occurred to Vincent again in Nuenen in 1884; once more the goal was to emulate the 'Black and Whites'. Vincent also recalled other British painters and in August he wrote to Theo, praising paintings by Constable and Millais that he remembered from the National Gallery and the Victoria & Albert Museum.

Paris and Arles

As we shall see in Chapter 4, Vincent knew several English-speaking painters and art dealers in Paris, including the Scotsman A.S. Hartrick, the Australian John Peter Russell (both of whom Vincent met through Cormon's *atelier*) and Hartrick's fellow Scot, Alexander Reid, who would play a vital role in introducing Post-Impressionism to Scotland.

In 1888, after only five months in Arles, Vincent considered returning to London with Goupil's to sell Impressionist art. Ultimately, however, he decided not to make the break. Nevertheless, he continued to incorporate references to English art and literature in his work. He remained a fervent admirer of the 'Black and Whites' and an avid reader of the novels of Charles Dickens. *Gauguin's Chair* (November 1888), featuring a lighted candle, recalled one of Luke Fildes's illustrations for Dickens's last novel, *Edwin Drood*, while *At Eternity's Gate* (May 1890) was inspired by one of A.B. Houghton's illustrations for *Hard Times*. It could be said that, through such works, the 'Black and Whites' had been translated into colour.

* * *SUMMARY* * *

• Having taken up drawing again in The Hague, Vincent kept up his pastime in England. The themes of his later art were inspired partly by English novels, poetry, illustration and painting.

• The definitive story of Vincent's love life in England may never be known. Whatever the truth of it, some personal crisis turned him towards religion, and by late 1876 Vincent was preaching sermons in and around Richmond, Surrey.

• Vincent taught languages and Bible study at schools in Ramsgate and Isleworth, and later at an English-run Sunday School in Amsterdam.

• Later in life, Vincent talked of returning to England to work as an illustrator or in an art gallery. But this was not to be.

4 Vincent the Painter

HORIZONS: THE RANGE OF VINCENT'S WORK

Vincent van Gogh's art embraces wide horizons – penetrating portraits of himself and others; vivid images of day and night; scenes of human activity and of close intimacy, and still lifes that glow with inner light. Whether painting the umber darkness of a Dutch peasant home, the white heat of Provence or the inspiring power of the cosmos, Van Gogh expresses an intense communion with his surroundings. And in his images of people, he conveys profound insights into the human condition.

Van Gogh painted approximately 40 self-portraits, three-quarters of these in Paris (1886–8), seven in Arles (1888–9) and four in St-Rémy (1889). Van Gogh's self-portraits are a visible indicator of changes in his art and in his own physical and mental state. Through colour, contour, line and texture, they convey a range of human emotions – from energy and self-assurance to anxiety and sadness. Never mere surface descriptions, they are images of the artist's soul and, as Vincent intended, the windows to that soul are the *eyes*. In the largest self-portrait, painted in the St-Rémy asylum and now displayed in the Musée d'Orsay in Paris, both the face and the background express the stormy landscape of the artist's mind.

Of Vincent's many portraits of other people, three (1887–8) are of **Julien 'Père' Tanguy**, the Paris dealer in **avant-garde** paintings and artists' materials. The first of these portraits parallels many of Vincent's Parisian self-portraits: a close scrutiny of the sitter's character, with the background defined only

KEYWORDS

'Père' Tanguy: a former member of the revolutionary Paris Commune (March–May 1871), who was a friend and supporter of many young artists.

Avant-garde: associated with the newest ideas.

Illustration 1 *Portrait of 'Père' Tanguy* (Musée Rodin, Paris)

Illustration 2   *The Potato Eaters* (Van Gogh Museum, Amsterdam)

by colour, shadow and brushwork. The second and third portraits of Tanguy are in striking contrast to this. A paternal-looking Tanguy, in boat-like straw hat, sits before a background of fashionable Japanese prints (see Illustration 1). Depicting trees in blossom, mountains and exotic headgear and with (to Western eyes) strange compositions, such colourful prints were avidly collected by Vincent, who adapted them to his own innovative purposes. Vincent's art found a loyal champion in 'Père' (Father) Tanguy, whose shop exhibited many of his paintings.

As rich with meaning as Van Gogh's many individual portraits, is a group portrait, *The Potato Eaters* (1885, see Illustration 2). Although Vincent had drawn groups of people in the Borinage mining district, *The Potato Eaters* (measuring 81.5 cm by 114.5 cm) was his first big, deliberately constructed composition of a group, and it is a moving tribute to the peasants of North Brabant. Here, members of the De Groot and Van Rooy families are seen in communion with each other and with their hard-earned food. Darkly atmospheric in the spirit of Rembrandt and painted nearly a year before Vincent's move to Paris, there is no sign in *The Potato Eaters* of the brilliant colour schemes to come. Rather, the colours are symbolic of earth and as Vincent suggested of his artist-hero Millet, the peasants seem to be painted *with* the earth that they sow with seed. *The Potato Eaters* evolved through at least 40 preparatory stages, including a lithograph (of which there are 17 known impressions). Having struggled to perfect the composition, Vincent sent the finished work to his brother Theo in Paris, but it was not until 1892 that it was shown in public in Amsterdam. *The Potato Eaters* embodies themes for which Vincent was to become famous: expressive portraits, evocative still-lifes, and the dramatic interplay of darkness and light.

TUITION: VINCENT THE STUDENT

Formal tuition

Childhood
In the vacuum between leaving his first school in 1861, aged eight, and going to boarding school in 1864, Van Gogh was educated by his parents; it was his mother – an accomplished artist in her own right – who encouraged him to draw. Some of Vincent's spirited drawings

KEYWORD

Old master: Painter acknowledged as a master of art and usually working before 1800.

from this early period survive, including sketches of a mug, a dog, a bridge and a barn. Later, at his third and final school, in Tilburg (September 1866 to March 1868) Vincent was to enjoy four hours a week of art lessons. Under the inspiring guidance of C.C. Huysmans, who had trained in Paris, Vincent gained his first, but by no means last, experience of drawing plaster casts of the human body and copying **old master** reproductions; Huysmans also encouraged him to draw directly from nature.

Brussels and The Hague
Although after leaving school, Vincent continued to draw and acquired an immense knowledge of the art scene by working at Goupil's, there was a break in his formal art tuition until the early 1880s. In Brussels,

1880–1, Vincent picked up useful hints from artists such as Van Rappard, who encouraged him to 'compose' groups of people; group compositions are an essential part of works like *The Potato Eaters*. More intensive tuition came from Vincent's cousin Anton Mauve, a leader of The Hague School of landscape artists in Holland. Mauve advised Vincent to broaden his media to include charcoal, black chalk and ink. He also gave him a paintbox, and taught him the principles of oil and watercolour; Vincent declared that with painting his real career would begin. Mauve also suggested that Vincent would benefit from more room to paint in and kindly lent him some money to set up a studio. Although he sometimes clashed with his tutor, Vincent learned a great deal from him and, when Mauve died in 1888 aged 50, Vincent dedicated a painting, *Pink Peach Trees*, to his memory. Since 1882, Vincent had, in his pictures, often underlined his name with a diagonal line, in homage to Mauve's own signature.

Antwerp

Vincent attended the Antwerp Academy from January/February 1886 and although he was taught painting by the Academy's Director, Charles Verlat, he became frustrated by his experiences there. While working conscientiously at copying plaster casts, he was equally determined to work from the live nude. To this end, he sought out a drawing club where he could draw live models. Vincent also rebelled against the Academy's drawing classes under Eugeen Siberdt (a tutor who seemed obsessed with exact detail) and determined to take a different route.

Paris

Vincent left for Paris in March 1886 and in the autumn enrolled as a student at the Montmartre *atelier* of Fernand Cormon. Cormon was an **academician** and no zealot for the new theories of art. But neither was he a blinkered conservative. His *atelier* was a magnet for young artists, including the head student,

KEYWORD

Academician: member of a prestigious Academy (Cormon belonged to the Institut Français).

Illustration 3 *Café Terrace at Night* (Kröller-Müller Museum, Otterlo)

Henri de Toulouse-Lautrec as well as Louis Anquetin, Emile Bernard and the rich Australian John Peter Russell (who knew Japan at first hand). Vincent got to know them well and for four months at Cormon's *atelier* he worked hard to improve his drawing and painting technique. At the same time he was absorbing a whole range of new ideas from the melting-pot of the contemporary art scene in Paris.

Self-tuition

Despite the formal tuition that Van Gogh received, he was basically self-taught. An intense observer of the world around him, he learnt by practice and a determination to improve. He portrayed miners at work in the Borinage and he drew the countryside and its local 'types' in Etten, Drenthe and Nuenen (where he painted *The Potato Eaters*). Helped by a printer in The Hague, and hoping to illustrate magazines, Vincent took up lithography and collected magazine wood-engravings. In museums, he scrutinized the paintings of old masters, for example, the emotionally-charged colour and brushwork of Rubens. Vincent was also absorbed by the power of the written word. He delved into the subject of colour, buying a copy of *Grammaire des Arts du Dessin* by Charles Blanc, former Director of the Ecole des Beaux Arts in Paris. Blanc had analysed the relationship between primaries (red, blue, yellow) and their contrasting complementaries (green, orange, violet) by way of a six-pointed star and the angles between the points. Vincent pushed this 'complementary contrast' to extremes, for

KEYWORD

Pendant: a painting designed to complement another and to be hung next to it.

instance, setting lurid reds against sickly greens in his sinister painting *The Night Café*. Another good example is *Harvest at La Crau* (see Illustration 4 for a study of the painting), with a turquoise sky that brings out the blues in the mountains, cart and shadows and complements the orange roofs. Its **pendant** was to be a painting of haystacks.

Teach yourself books

Van Gogh used teach yourself books to improve his technique. In 1879–80, while living in the Borinage district, he copied plaster casts and old master drawings from Charles Bargue's *Drawing Course* and, in 1881, while living with his parents in Etten, he studied Bargue's *Charcoal Exercises* which offered step-by-step progress in figure drawing. Vincent used what he learnt from Bargue's books to draw and paint local 'types' – diggers, sweepers, growers and ploughmen – and was not too proud to refer to Bargue whenever he felt the need.

Illustration 4 *Harvest at La Crau* (Fogg Art Museum, Harvard University. A pen and watercolour study for the oil painting in the Van Gogh Museum, Amsterdam)

WAYS AND MEANS: TOOLS OF THE TRADE

The vast *oeuvre* of Vincent van Gogh that survives, consists of over 2000 paintings, drawings and prints – a phenomenal contribution to the story of art. Vincent made his indelible mark through a whole range of artists' media.

'Essentials' among Vincent's 'tools of the trade' include the following.

Black chalk
A powerful medium for dramatic line and contour that Vincent used in *Sorrow* (1882, his deeply sad portrayal of Sien, his girlfriend and model), and in his drawings of the peasants of Nuenen.

> **KEYWORD**
> *Mistral*: violent wind in southern France.

Brushes
Self-Portrait in Front of the Easel (Paris, early 1888) shows Vincent holding a brilliant palette of colour and a range of brushes in various sizes. The extremely varied character of Vincent's brushwork shows the many styles with which he engaged, including Pointillism and, in contrast, the flat, bold colour of Japanese prints. He could wield the brush to echo the movement of the scene before him, as with a turbulent, **mistral**-driven sky in *Wheat Field with Cypresses* (1889).

Canvas and paper
Vincent normally cut his own linen canvas from rolls ready-primed by his suppliers and nailed it to the frame, although he also experimented with a coarser (and cheaper) jute canvas during his collaboration with Gauguin (October to December 1888). Vincent's paintings come in a wide range of sizes, but many from the South of France are 'size 30' (roughly 70 cm by 90 cm), including *Irises, The Starry Night* (both 1889), and the three versions (the first in October 1888) of *Vincent's Bedroom at Arles*. Types of paper that Vincent used for drawing and watercolour included the 'double Ingres', a textured paper of double thickness.

Colour
As we have seen, Vincent put to radical use the theory of complementary contrast, for example red against green or blue against orange. As a body of work, his paintings embrace the full spectrum of colour from vermilion to violet. Whether conveying moods of happiness, stress, danger, purity or rest, Vincent uses colour in ways that are deeply expressive.

Frames
Vincent thought very carefully about the colour of his picture frames, having in mind a specific function in relation to the picture. Thus he

used white for his 'Bedroom' paintings (for contrast, there is no white in the picture); orange for an 1890 painting of cypress trees (to complement the 'tartan' colour effect of the painting); yellow (to emphasize the brilliant tones of *Lemons, Pears, Apples, Grapes and an Orange* (1887). He asked for *The Potato Eaters* to be framed in gold, to enhance the highlights thrown by the oil lamp.

Ink
Sometimes Vincent applied black or sepia ink with brush (on occasion diluting the ink with turpentine), but usually with pens – both steel (*Pollard Birches*, 1884) and 'Japanese' reed pens, which he made himself.

Oil paint
Vincent used oil paint from various sources, including the Paris colourmen Tasset & l'Hôte and 'Père' Tanguy, but oil paint was by no means free of problems. Some of Tasset & l'Hôte's pigments were ground so finely that they came out of the tube too oily; Vincent estimated that an 1890 painting of cypresses would take a year to dry thoroughly. Sometimes Vincent used **fugitive** or unstable colours. For example, a type of red called 'lake' fades over time, which is why some pinks in Vincent's

KEYWORD

Fugitive: not light-fast, i.e. prone to fading.

paintings can no longer be seen. However, with oil paint he could build up a thick impasto to convey atmosphere (*Wheatfield with Cypresses*) and texture, notably in the *Sunflower* paintings and to evoke the spiritual auras around sun, moon and stars.

Perspective frame
In one of Vincent's seven surviving sketchbooks there is a drawing of a perspective frame; Vincent often used such a frame to ensure accurate landscape perspective. Such frames were used as far back as the Renaissance, for example by the German artist, Albrecht Dürer (1471–1528).

Watercolour
This was originally taught to Vincent by his cousin, Anton Mauve. He also used *gouache* ('body colour'), which is watercolour made opaque

by adding white pigment. One of Vincent's best watercolours is *The State Lottery Office*, painted in The Hague in 1882. This image had a particular significance for him, since Carolien Haanebeek (see page 29) worked there.

Through these 'tools of the trade' Vincent developed one of the most distinctive styles in the history of art. In the mind's eye we can visualize him in the white heat of Provence, painting for up to 16 hours a day, his easel fixed down with iron pegs against the *mistral* wind, and coping with the mosquitoes and flies and the radiant, but relentless, sun.

VINCENT AND EXHIBITIONS

Van Gogh took part in several major exhibitions from 1888, but 1887 was notable for some smaller-scale shows in which he was a prime mover. The Café du Tambourin and the Restaurant du Chalet (a *Grand Bouillon* or Big Eating House), situated respectively on the Boulevard and Avenue de Clichy to the south and west of Montmartre, were a rendezvous for artists and writers and places where they could exhibit.

In the Tambourin, Vincent organized an exhibition of the popular Japanese prints which helped to shape the style of much of the new art. He also showed his own work there, as did Toulouse-Lautrec.

In the Chalet, Vincent set up an exhibition of artists at the cutting edge who had not yet achieved the status of those such as Monet and Renoir. Vincent called these rising stars the 'Impressionists of the Petit [Small] Boulevard'. However, the show's profile could be described as Post-Impressionist and apart from Vincent himself, there were Toulouse-Lautrec and the leaders of the **Cloisonnists**, Louis Anquetin and Emile Bernard. Bernard reckoned that Vincent had about 100 pictures there; thus the show had Vincent's unmistakable 'stamp' and it gave him a chance to discuss his work with fellow artists, including Gauguin and Seurat.

KEYWORD

Cloisonnists: group of painters inspired by the structure and colour of medieval stained glass and enamel.

Through two other exhibitions, Vincent made contact with leaders of the theatrical and literary avant-garde. The first was in the rehearsal room and foyer of the ultra-modernist Théâtre Libre, run by the innovative producer André Antoine. Vincent shared this exhibition with two other artists at the cutting edge of innovation, Seurat and Signac. The second exhibition took place in the offices of the Revue Indépendante, a **Symbolist** journal co-founded by the critic and anarchist Félix Fénéon. Fénéon was a fanatical supporter of the new art, and in a sketch now in the Ashmolean Museum, Oxford in England, Lucien Pissarro drew Vincent and Fénéon in earnest conversation.

KEYWORDS

Symbolists: painters whose style used colour, line and the subject itself to evoke ideas.

Retrospective: exhibition looking back on an artist's career.

There were two large-scale avenues for publicizing Vincent's paintings. First, the Independents' Salon (founded in opposition to the official Salon in 1884) and second, the Salon of 'Les Vingt' (The Twenty), founded by Belgian modernists whose exhibitions were international.

Vincent's work 'hung' at three Independents' Salons. At the last, in March 1890 and only four months before he died, he showed ten paintings and achieved, according to Pissarro and Gauguin, a huge success with his fellow-artists.

In November 1889, Vincent sent six paintings to Brussels for hanging at the seventh Salon of 'Les Vingt', which opened the following January. The contrasting works, hung in a group, included two of the *Sunflowers* (one of which is now in the National Gallery, London); *Ivy* (May 1889, now lost); *Orchard in Bloom* (April 1889); *Wheat Field at Sunrise*, and *The Red Vineyard*. Only *The Red Vineyard* found a buyer.

In the years immediately after Vincent's death, two of his artist friends organized small exhibitions of his work in Paris: Paul Signac at the March 1891 Independents' Salon; and Emile Bernard in April 1892 at Le Barc de Boutteville's Gallery, where he showed 16 of Vincent's paintings. By the year's end, the first large **retrospective**, in Amsterdam, signalled Van Gogh's public elevation to the status of an icon.

SALES: EXCEPTIONS THAT PROVED THE RULE?

Contrary to the romantic image of the artist, driven only by the passionate will to create, sales were important to Van Gogh. Although, during his lifetime, he did not find many buyers, it is recorded that:

* Vincent sold 22 drawings in 1882 to his uncle Cornelis Marinus (CM) van Gogh, an art dealer.

* Hermanus Tersteeg, Vincent's boss at Goupil's in The Hague, bought one drawing.

* Vincent was paid for a portrait of one of 'Père' Tanguy's friends and 'Mère' Tanguy sold a portrait that Vincent had painted of her, so glad was she to see the back of it.

* A still life of shrimps was sold to a small Parisian art dealer.

* Vincent sold a self-portrait to Sulley & Lori, art dealers from London.

* The critic Albert Aurier bought, from Theo, several works from Vincent's Dutch period.

* *The Red Vineyard* was bought at the Salon of 'Les Vingt' in January 1890 by the 'Vingt-iste' Anna Boch, who paid 400 Belgian francs for it, the highest price paid for one of Vincent's pictures during his lifetime.

In addition to these sales, Vincent also exchanged his paintings with other artists, for food (for example, at Le Tambourin), for painting materials at Tanguy's shop and for money. Thus, Theo agreed in 1884 to a form of 'contract' whereby he would pay Vincent a generous 150 francs a month in exchange for his paintings, which Theo would then try to sell.

The huge auction prices, £25 million and upwards, that Van Gogh's paintings would one day command, lay a century in the future.

DEFINING VAN GOGH

As we have seen, Van Gogh's art did not belong to a single style or 'school'. Rather like a planet being formed, his painting 'character' evolved as elements fused together. And the intriguing question remains, as it does for all creators who die young, what further changes might have occurred had he lived?

Conventionally, Vincent has been described as a Post-Impressionist, one of those who sought a deeper or more strictly 'scientific' art than that practised by Renoir and his Impressionist colleagues. More recently the term 'Pre-Expressionist' has been used to stress Vincent's stylistic and spiritual connections with later German **Expressionism**. That he inspired the Expressionists of the future is true, but Vincent also looked to the great art of the past for

KEYWORD

Expressionism: art which is not 'strictly' realistic but could be said to be 'more truthful than the truth' (Van Gogh's phrase). It derives from the artist's emotional response to reality.

inspiration and he held fast to his heroes, including Rembrandt (1606–69) and Meissonier (1815–91), a technically brilliant but much maligned French painter.

Nevertheless, Vincent did embrace, and make highly personal, Post-Impressionist theories and styles, one of which was Symbolism. Indeed, Vincent's art is rich in symbolic images or 'emblems': sunflowers (good), sowers (life), reapers (death) and the sun (the creator). As A. M. & R. Hammacher have written, Vincent was 'abnormally sensitive to symbols'.

Even so, however interesting it may be to look for artistic connections, this does not really do justice to Vincent van Gogh. For Vincent was a self-defining genius, and in that lies his crown.

* * * SUMMARY * * *

● Vincent van Gogh was a prolific artist and the range of his subjects is immense. Whatever he painted, he evoked its spirit and not just its form.

● In portraits Vincent explored human character and his self-portraits reflect the experiences of a changing self.

● Stylistically, Vincent was a bold experimenter, receptive to artistic influences, yet in the final analysis 'his own man'. He also used a wide range of media, but he is most celebrated for his oil paintings.

● His handling of colour shows an imaginative command of the spectrum. As with much of his subject matter, colour was used symbolically to convey a meaning, and not merely to describe.

● Vincent had ambitious artistic goals – to convey truth, compassion, creation and renewal. A thread of spiritual imagery is to be found throughout his painting career.

● Vincent sometimes painted different versions of the same *motif* (theme): Sunflowers in a vase (at least four); his bedroom in Arles (three); Wheat field with cypresses (two); the self-portraits (around 40).

● Vincent received some significant formal tuition but was, for the most part, self-taught. He never stopped learning.

● He had a profound gift of communication, through his art and his letters.

● Vincent's output represents a rich harvest of images, the seeds sown in childhood and brought to maturity by his fertile imagination.

Vincent the Writer 5

INTRODUCTION

Vincent van Gogh wrote sermons and it has been speculated that he may have kept a diary. However, it is thanks to the letters he wrote that a literary self-portrait has been bequeathed to posterity. Although many of his letters were subsequently edited or destroyed by their recipients – for example, by members of his own family in order to censor an unfortunate episode, or (in one case) burnt by the Teersteg family in order to make a fire to warm a sitting-room on a cold day – about 900 letters, written between 1872 and 1890, have survived.

Even before the first edition in 1914 of *Letters to his Brother*, supervized by his sister-in-law, Johanna van Gogh-Bonger, Vincent's letters were already a piece of history charting the development of Vincent the individual and the changing cultural and social contexts with which he engaged. He dissects human character and experience, and the situations that help to shape them. Vincent reflects on his progress as an artist and the people and places that inspired him – in so doing, he draws on an awesome range of artistic and literary references.

A creative medium in their own right, Vincent's letters express his mind and soul as forcefully as his art; truly, one may speak here of the art of letter-writing. A vast 650 of the letters, some of them 5,000 words long, are to his brother and financial lifeline, Theo van Gogh. Several of Vincent's letters to his parents and sister Wil (Willemina) survive, as do a number to friends in Arles, and to the artists Rappard, Russell (the Australian whom Vincent had befriended in Paris), Gauguin and Signac. Some of the first to be read by the public were to the Post-Impressionist painter Emile Bernard, who in 1893 made the decision to publish them. With many of his letters Vincent included intriguing sketches (about 200 in all) of paintings and drawings he was working on. Some of these sketches were photographed by Picasso's girlfriend, Dora Maar, for the 1938 edition of Vincent's letters to Bernard, translated by Douglas Lord.

Generally speaking, Vincent wrote in his own impressionistic form of Dutch when writing from the Netherlands, Belgium and England, and in French when living in France, 1886–90. However, he also wrote letters in English to John Peter Russell and to Harry Gladwell, and presumably to Alex Reid and Reverend T. Slade-Jones, and he would insert English phrases into his Dutch and French correspondence, such as 'Lord, keep my memory green!' (L120*). Whatever his chosen language, Vincent sometimes underlined words for emphasis, though recent analysis suggests much of this underlining was by a later hand. Vincent's handwriting itself often reflects a highly emotional state of mind.

Academic research on his correspondence continues apace. Although Vincent did not generally date his letters, the work of several generations of Van Gogh experts had, by the mid-1980s established a revised and credible sequence. Scholarly commentaries in English enhance the 1963 (Roskill) and 1996 (de Leeuw & Pomerans) selections of Vincent's letters. On the centenary of Vincent's death, in 1990, came a fully revised collected edition in four volumes, with sections restored where Johanna had earlier edited them or excised them altogether – such as the reference to Dorus van Gogh's plan in 1881 to send his son to a humane psychiatric hospital in Belgium.

Since 1990, things have moved on again. The present Van Gogh Letters Project (generated in Amsterdam and The Hague) is a huge endeavour involving a team of scholars and translators. The new edition, due to appear c.2010, will be a multi-volume work, fully annotated with footnotes and expert comment; Vincent's letters will appear in the original languages that Vincent used, as well as in English translation.

What can we learn from Vincent's letters?

VINCENT: HIS INNER BEING

Health

'For days my mind has been wandering wildly … I apparently pick up dirt from the ground and eat it.'

St-Rémy, August 1889
(L601*)

Vincent's letters tell us that he experienced vertigo and extreme fatigue and that he suffered from insomnia, a weak stomach, bad teeth, melancholy, neurosis, gonorrhoea and a form of epilepsy. It is clear from reading the letters that Vincent could articulate his experiences clearly and objectively; he did not confuse delirium and reality. From St-Rémy, for example, he wrote that during his outbreaks of illness his sense of time and space became distorted, with people and voices coming to him from a great distance, 'and to be *quite different* from what they are in reality' (to his sister Wil, October 1889, W15). But such traumas did not blunt Vincent's zest for life; indeed, in the face of physical and mental adversity he demonstrated formidable resilience.

To what did Vincent attribute his illness? In April 1889 he admitted that it was something of an occupational hazard: that he and the painters with whom he identified ('we other painters', L588*) were ripe for the asylum. He further believed that his neurosis was partly 'a fatal inheritance, since in civilisation the weakness increases from generation to generation' (to Theo, Arles, May 1888, L481). The times in which he lived also had much to answer for: 'We are exposed to the conditions and illnesses of our age' (L595*). By September 1889, Vincent was resigned to his 'attacks', and around 10 July 1890 (a fortnight before his death), he wrote to Theo and Jo van Gogh, 'My life is also under attack at its very root' (L649*).

What remedies did Vincent follow? In July 1889 he wrote to Theo that for nearly six months he had cut right down on his drinking and smoking. To help to overcome his insomnia, he put camphor oil on his pillow, and it is possible that, to '[purify] the blood' (L489*), i.e. to kill bacteria, he took potassium iodide. He believed in, but did not always practice, a balanced regimen: 'To do good work one must eat well, be well housed, have one's fling from time to time, smoke one's pipe and drink one's coffee in peace' (To Emile Bernard, Arles, September 1888, B17). As a deterrent to suicide, Vincent followed Charles Dickens's prescription: a glass of wine, a piece of bread and cheese, and a pipe of tobacco. In the asylum at St-Rémy (1889–90), he took hydropathic baths. However, as early as 1882 Vincent had written to Theo from The Hague that the best remedy for ill health was to paint!

When he arrived in Arles from Paris in February 1888, Vincent was physically weak, but by mid-August he wrote that his stomach had recovered and that the heat of the southern summer had restored him. He could write to Gauguin of energy so tremendous that 'my bony carcass makes straight for its [artistic] objective. The result is a degree of sincerity, perhaps original at times, about what I feel' (October 1888, L544a*). Although at the young age of 29 he had written to Theo that he had wrinkles on his brow and lines in his face, looked 40 and – in an ironic pass at the landscape that he loved – had hands that were 'full of furrows', Vincent also showed that he could bounce back.

Character, personality and moods

Vincent's letters are testimony to the fact that his melancholy was balanced by a strong streak of optimism, his seriousness by a cutting sense of humour, and his directness by a heavy dose of irony. From the Borinage in July 1880 he wrote of his family to Theo, that they had 'perhaps never been wholly weaned from prejudice and other equally honourable and respectable qualities' (L133*). Concerning the family quarrel over his relationship with a prostitute, Vincent asked them not to cut his head off – he still needed it for drawing! (to Theo, The Hague, May 1882, L98*). Nevertheless, Vincent did not bear grudges; alhough wounded by Rappard's attack in June 1885 on his lithograph of *The Potato Eaters*, Vincent invited him to work in his studio and in fact they continued to correspond for some months. Enclosed with

Vincent's last letter to Rappard were some bird's nests, sent for Rappard to copy.

Vincent wrote frequently of his progress as an artist and how it helped to build character. 'Taking things lying down is what I did in years gone by; taking action and being alert is what I do now, having found my work and my vocation' (to Theo, The Hague, May 1882, L98*). His letters speak of strong will-power and resolve: from Amsterdam in April 1878, Vincent wrote to Theo of the merits of leading an upright life and refusing to be crushed by setbacks; that way one was worth more than the person who had it easy … one should keep one's inner fire alight!

These assertive traits found their reverse, however, in elements of resignation and self-criticism. Admitted to St Paul's asylum in St-Rémy, he wrote that he was resigned to being an outsider, 'to living under surveillance, even if it is sympathetic, and to sacrifice one's liberty, to remain outside society with nothing but one's work as distraction' (to Theo, May 1889, L631*). In the early 1880s Vincent had written frankly of his own imperfections as an artist, while from Arles in early 1889 he expressed remorse for Gauguin's departure and for the failure of the 'Studio of the South'.

From his letters, Vincent's modesty is strongly evident. He called his career as a painter 'humble' and within the profession saw himself as a secondary figure compared to Gauguin and Monticelli. Yes, he said, he could paint cypresses and olive trees, but their symbolic language should be conveyed by artists more capable than he. Vincent's modesty was linked to a keen intelligence and he wrote to Rappard in March 1884 that technique should be so skilful that it is not seen as technique. 'Let our work … not reek of our cleverness …' (R43*). Vincent did not feel he was yet that good an artist. He condemned immodesty in others, albeit with a poetic subtlety. 'And not being too troubled by our weaknesses, for even he who has none, has one weakness, namely that he has none …' (to Theo, Amsterdam, April 1878, L121*).

Beliefs, philosophy of life and values

For generations, the Van Gogh family had been closely associated with the Church, but what was the place of religion in Vincent's personal life? Although traumas in love may have affected him deeply, it seems it was the melancholy and alienation that Vincent experienced during his posting to Goupil's in Paris (May 1875 to March 1876) that led him to seek personal fulfilment in religion – and a particularly exacting, even masochistic, form at that.

By July 1875, the religious references in Vincent's letters were frequent. Vincent tells Theo he will soon be sending him a French Bible and a copy of Thomas à Kempis's *Imitation of Christ*; in August he quotes the texts of sermons he has heard in Paris, including 'Happy are they for whom life is all thorns', and in the same letter, 'Fear God and keep his commandments' (L34). In September Vincent tells Theo to read only the Bible, and he asks God to 'teach us to deny ourselves, to take [up] our cross every day...' (L39b). A philosophy of self-denial, suffering and pushing himself to the limit would continue to colour Vincent's brief life on earth.

When teaching at Reverend Slade-Jones's school in Isleworth, Vincent's religious fervour was palpable. 'I want' he wrote to Theo in August 1876, 'to be bound to Christ with unbreakable bonds, and to feel these bonds. To be sorrowful yet always rejoicing' (L74*). With his letter to Theo of 31 October 1876, Vincent enclosed the text of his first sermon in English. In it he expressed his belief that embracing Christ throughout life could make life 'evergreen' (enclosed with L79*); the sermon is rich in images of working for such a fruitful life – furrowing with the plough, fishing with the net. Living the godly life is difficult, like weathering a stormy sea, but it is important to humankind to seek to grow better in our progress on life's pilgrimage. 'We may not live on just anyhow' (enclosed with L79*).

Vincent's letters to Theo in the late 1870s express a deep faith in God's power to renew the soul, and he saw the word of God as a protective cloak against the storms of life. Indeed, as he was to write in November 1881, in taking necessary risks, in putting out to sea, there is 'safety in the very heart of danger' (L156*).

Yet Vincent's spiritual connection with the Church was not to last. In December 1881, having a bitter confrontation with his parents and Uncle Stricker (a priest, like Vincent's father) over his love for his cousin, Kee Vos, Vincent became deeply disillusioned and referred disparagingly to the clergy: '[their] **Jesuitisms** no longer have any hold on me now

KEYWORD

Jesuitisms: intrigues or equivocations ('necessary' lying).

Orders: classes of society.

… I believe in life and something real' (L164*), and he regretted he had 'allowed mystical and theological profundities to mislead me into withdrawing too much into myself' (L164*).

However, although Vincent may have abandoned the Church as an institution, he did not turn his back on Christ. He retained a 'code of life' based on personal rules (which he distinguished from rules invented by others), remaining committed to turning these principles into action.

Valuing individuals for their worth rather than their wealth, he felt empathy for the poor. Pondering his family's disapproval of his relationships with those 'beneath' him, Vincent wrote, 'I don't have a great deal of thought to the question of lower or upper **orders**' (to Theo, Nuenen, March 1884, L358*). Despite conflicts within the family, Vincent was distressed when they became ill and, conscious of the strains in Theo's own life, felt rather guilty that he had to rely on Theo to keep him in paints and canvas. (As it happened, Theo himself was to die aged 33 in January 1891. He had been suffering from syphilis and kidney disease.)

In his letters, Vincent often expressed a deeply held wish to be of *use*. He valued commitment in relationships and wrote to Theo that it melted his heart when he felt compelled, in September 1883, to leave his prostitute girlfriend Sien and make for the wild landscapes of Drenthe. Vincent's sense of duty applied to art and artists; he believed in accomplishing great things in art (which he distinguished from 'ambition') and in 'self-control and willpower, sustained by one inspiring idea' (to Theo, August 1883, L309*). On the other hand, Vincent himself was open-minded and he baulked at narrowness in others. He advised Emile Bernard to respect artists who were different from himself, otherwise he would become like those 'who utterly despise all others and believe themselves to be the only just ones' (B1). From Arles in 1888 he told his sister Wil, 'It is not right to know only one thing – one gets stultified by that; one should not rest before one knows the opposite too' (W4). And, once having started to look at things with an open mind, one should not 'backslide' into prejudice (to Theo, Amsterdam, April 1878, L121*).

VINCENT: HIS CREATIVE PROCESS

As with his paintings, Vincent could cast a spell with words. At times he seems to have created a new form of expression in the way he fuses the visual and the literary 'image'. In a beautiful example of such a word painting, Vincent described for Theo the village of Zweelo in Drenthe.

> 'Tones in the moss of gold-green, in the ground of reddish or bluish or yellowish dark lilac-greys, tones of inexpressible purity in the green of the little cornfields, tones of black in the wet tree trunks, standing out against the golden rain of swirling, teeming autumn leaves ... The sky smooth and bright, shining, not white but a barely detectable lilac, white vibrant with red, blue and yellow, reflecting everything and felt everywhere above one, hazy and merging with the thin mist below, fusing everything in a gamut of delicate greys.'
>
> To Theo, Drenthe, November 1883
> (L340*)

Not only do Vincent's letters express the poetic soul of the countryside, but they also offer a dramatic sense of the physical act of painting. To his mother, he wrote in October 1889 that, just as peasants ploughed their fields, so also he ploughed his canvases, as if painting were a three, rather than a two-dimensional process. Similarly when describing the physical structure of a painting, he wrote that it should have clearly defined **planes**: the first (to the rear) was the really essential one, for without this solid foundation the painting would lack depth and things would come 'too much to the forefront' (to Rappard, 1884, R46).

KEYWORDS

planes: 'layers' in the composition of a picture, which lend depth from background to foreground.

lithographic stone: stone onto which the design for a lithographic print is drawn.

Whatever the medium – for example, paint or lithography – the artist should be true to it, and not try false effects. Writing to Rappard in 1883, Vincent noted that a friend of Rappard's was trying to use a 'little pen' on a **lithographic stone**: 'Very fine pens, like very elegant people, are sometimes amazingly useless' (R30). One medium Vincent felt damaging to art, was photography, which he described as giving a 'dead' effect. Art should give impassioned expression to the true character rather than restate what the human eye through the camera lens could merely 'see'.

That Vincent, physically and psychologically, engaged with the subject and the medium as he painted, is conveyed in this fiery passage from a letter he wrote to Emile Bernard from Arles (April 1888):

'I hit the canvas with irregular touches of the brush, which I leave as they are. Patches of thickly laid-on colour, spots of canvas left uncovered, here and there portions that are left absolutely unfinished, repetitions, savageries ...'

(B3)

Vincent's letters offer rich insights into his use of colour: 'By intensifying *all* the colours one arrives once again at quietude and harmony ... There are colours which cause each other to shine brilliantly, which form a *couple*, which complete each other like man and woman' (to Wil, mid-Summer 1888, W3 and W4). But the demands of balancing primary and secondary colours could lead to serious mental strain. Vincent wrote to Bernard that the process of painting *La Mousmé* (the daughter of the Ginoux family, who ran the Café de la Gare in Arles) with its red, blue, yellow (primary) and green, orange, and 'lilac' (secondary) had so exhausted him that he could hardly write.

KEYWORDS

La Mousmé: originally a young Japanese girl.

Nevertheless, to Vincent the power of colour to evoke atmosphere and express character was undeniable. For the background to his portrait of the Belgian artist Eugène Boch, Vincent used 'the richest, most intense blue I can contrive' (L520*) to paint infinity (Boch's dreams). Vincent again used blue to dramatic effect in *Café Terrace at Night*, 1888 (Illustration 3, p.41) – a night scene without any black, 'done with nothing but beautiful blue and violet and green, and in these surroundings the lighted square acquires a pale sulphur and greenish citron-yellow colour' (to Wil, September 1888, W7).

Painting the olive trees at St-Rémy was a complex process: 'They are silvery, sometimes more blue, sometimes whitish and bronze green, against a yellow, purple-pink or orange to dull red-ochre ground' (to Theo, Autumn 1889, L608*). More than a year before, Vincent had written, 'The painter of the future will be a colourist the like of which has never yet been seen' (L482*). By the Autumn of 1889, he himself was that painter.

'Art is jealous, she doesn't like taking second place to an indisposition.'

To Theo, July 1882
(L218*)

Why was art so important to Vincent? He felt that its fundamental purpose was, like music, to restore and comfort the living. But Vincent also wished his art to reveal *truths* to both present and future generations, about nature and about humanity. Concerning his own *oeuvre*, Vincent felt it crucial that it should be judged as a whole. Using an ingenious analogy, he compared individual works to a series of blocks seen in perspective. The near end of a block will be seen larger than the far end and it joins to the 'short' end of the next block. But if you remove one block, you will be judging the art work out of context and deny that the artist's output is a developing whole (to Theo, August 1883).

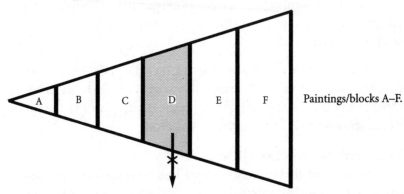

Paintings/blocks A–F.

If D is removed, you take it out of context and diminish its creator.

In 1885, Vincent wrote about himself as a *modern* artist because he did something neither the Greeks nor Renaissance artists nor the Dutch old masters had done, which was to paint peasant figures in action. He also did not moralize in his paintings. In 1888, he also identified expressive portraiture as the art of the present and future; because he was a humanitarian and a colourist he could make a personal contribution to this **genre**. His portraits of the gardener, Patience Escalier, and of Lieutenant Milliet, from Arles, show the truth of this statement.

KEYWORD

Genre: type of subject – landscape, nude, battle scene, etc.

But could the modern artist succeed in isolation? He wrote to Emile Bernard twice extolling the virtues of the fraternal **collective** of artists in September 1888. The collective's members would, he explained to Theo soon after arriving in Arles, still maintain their individual prestige by giving a certain number

> **KEYWORD**
>
> Collective: co-operative association practising the principle of equality and mutual help.

of their own pictures to the group each year for sale, so that every member could go on living and working. The intensively creative (but ultimately destructive) partnership with Gauguin was the nearest Vincent got to realizing his dream of an artistic collective. He and Gauguin were 'pioneers' of the South, which Vincent saw as an aesthetic frontier.

Recovering in January 1889 after severing his left earlobe, Vincent wrote that he would not be able 'to reach the heights to which the illness to some extent led me' (L570*). However, the masterpieces of the future would show that Vincent's summit lay ahead.

VINCENT: HIS REFLECTIONS

Vincent believed that reflection was a healthy pursuit and his letters show that he himself reflected a great deal on the individual and on relationships, on the present and the future, on nature and on art and literature.

Reflecting on an individual's strength of character, Vincent wrote that attainment, independence and a code of conduct were important factors in character-building (to Theo, Amsterdam, April 1878). However, 'complying with and conforming to one thing today and another tomorrow, as the world dictates, by never contradicting the world and by heeding public opinion' was the quickest route to mediocrity (to Theo, Nuenen, December 1883, L347*).

Vincent reflected warmly on his brotherly friendship with Theo, writing to him that he valued it deeply and that Theo's visit to see him in the Borinage (August 1879) had made life feel 'good and precious' again. Yet reflections on relationships could also turn sour. In March 1884, walking alone, Vincent brooded on Theo's failure to sell his pictures and came for a while to see him as 'Father II', a latent source of conflict.

Vincent's reflections on love showed similar contrasts. He could write, 'There is the same difference between someone who is in love and what he was like before as there is between a lamp that is lit and one that is not … [in love] one has more peace of mind about many things and so is more likely to do better work' (to Theo, The Hague, March 1883, L276*). On the other hand, in 1887 he wrote from Paris to Theo, who was then in Holland, 'It was **Richepin** who said somewhere: the love of art is the undoing of true love. I think that's absolutely right but on the other hand true love makes one weary of art' (L462*). Vincent's ambivalent feelings at this time are clear from what he wrote to Wil, that the 'unsuitable' love affairs he was still

KEYWORD

Richepin: Jean Richepin (1849–1926). Prolific French poet and author associated with the Chat Noir cabaret.

having were 'absolutely right' because in the past, when he should have been in love, he was preoccupied with religion and 'socialist affairs' (W1*).

How did Vincent reflect on the *present* and the *future*? In 1886, he conjectured that, should there be a revolution at the end of the nineteenth century, then the reforms which followed would come too late for his generation to enjoy: 'We shall certainly <u>not</u> live to see the better lives when the air is clear and all society refreshed' (to Theo, Antwerp, early 1886, L451*). Two years later his prognosis for civilization was less hopeful, though not despairing. Now he returned to the theme of revolution and linked it with war and 'the bankruptcy of worm-eaten states' as disasters for the modern world. Out of this upheaval, however, might spring a new religion, 'consoling … making life possible, as the Christian religion used to' (to Theo, September 1888, L542*).

Ten years before, in the Borinage, Christianity had been uppermost in Vincent's mind. Reflecting on nature in a letter to Theo, he compared blackthorn hedges in the snow to the print on a page of the Gospel. Later when meditating on the landscape of Drenthe, Vincent was overwhelmed by the power of 'infinite' earth and sky, in the presence of which men and horses seemed no bigger than fleas (to Theo, November 1883, L340*).

In Amsterdam (1877–8), Vincent had used images from nature to encourage him in his difficult studies for the priesthood; reflecting on the steady growth of ivy along a wall, he saw its advance as a hopeful symbol of his own progress. As an artist, Vincent took up the challenge of making sense of nature so that he could interpret it clearly on paper and canvas. In the Autumn of 1881 (when he was in love with Kee Vos) he wrote to Theo that initially nature always resisted but, 'if [the artist] really takes her seriously he will not be put off by that opposition, on the contrary, it is all the more incentive to win her over' (L152*). With Kee he failed, but with nature he triumphed.

Nevertheless, the representation of natural forms raised interesting questions. How important, for example, was anatomical precision when representing human beings? Dry analysis of form, Vincent believed, did not make for true *art*. A truth greater that 'reality' could be achieved if artists painted things as they felt them to be – which Vincent had just done in his recently-completed *The Potato Eaters* (April 1885). As Vincent related in a letter to Rappard in March 1884, 'Art ... is not wrought by hands alone, but wells up from a deeper source, from man's soul' (R43*).

In turn, perfection in art was a means to a yet higher end: 'Anything complete and perfect renders infinity tangible, and the enjoyment of any beautiful thing is like coitus, a moment of infinity' (to Bernard, Arles, July 1888, B12).

What, then, was the highest attainment of art? Although he had long left his religious obsessions behind him, Vincent could still write to Emile Bernard in June 1888, that Christ was 'a greater artist than all the other artists, despising marble and clay as well as colour, working in living flesh.' It was Christ who 'made living men, immortals', and Christ who said 'Heaven and earth shall pass away but my words shall not pass away.' For Vincent, the immortal sayings of Christ were 'the very highest summit reached by art' (B8), and with that belief, Vincent reconciled the two forces – religion and art – that had most powerfully shaped his own life.

* * *SUMMARY* * *

● Vincent's letters, 1872–90, reveal his evolution as an artist and his pilgrimage through life.

● They engage the reader in the creative process and are a guide to understanding what makes good, and bad, art.

● Vincent's sayings still speak to us today and his 'code of life' is as relevant for our own times as it was for his.

● The letters show Vincent to be a man of principle yet, ultimately, free from rigid dogma.

● From the letters, Vincent's shining humanity emerges, as well as his profound artistic ideals.

'There are so many people, especially among comrades, who imagine that words are nothing – on the contrary, isn't it true that saying a thing well is as interesting and as difficult as painting it?'

To Bernard, April, 1888
(B4)

6 Perceptions of Van Gogh

IN THE MIRROR: HOW VINCENT SAW HIMSELF

The written impressions that Vincent conveyed of himself ranged from the confident to the wretched, from the crestfallen to the elated. At times he proclaimed his artistic mission, at others he was pessimistic about his talent and anxious when his contemporaries seemed indifferent.

Vincent's inner and outer selves, and the connections between them are also revealed in his self-portraits. Significantly, the very first that he painted in Paris is, in its composition (with Vincent posed at an easel) and in its dark tones, reminiscent of a self-portrait by one of his heroes, Rembrandt. It shows Vincent still in touch with an older Dutch school of painting. The term 'harmonist' has been used by Druick and Zegers (see Further Reading section) to describe Vincent's concern here with *tonal* harmony. In contrast, his last Paris self-portrait (also at the easel), is painted with a bright palette. Alongside Vincent's flower studies and his urban and rural landscapes at this time, this self-portrait shows how Van Gogh had, without abandoning harmony, now identified himself as a 'colourist'. This was a crucial development that doubled the 'firepower' of his artistic expression.

The significance of Vincent's manifesto pictures as 'testaments of the self' was discussed in Chapter 2. To these can be added the autobiographical *Van Gogh's Chair* of 1888 (acquired by the National Gallery in London in 1924, when it became one of the first paintings by Vincent to enter a public collection in Britain). The chair is modest, sturdy, gnarled. On the rush seat lies Vincent's pipe and tobacco, in its paper wrap, waiting to be smoked in peace. The chair looks simple in itself, but in its interaction with other elements, such as the floor tiles, it presents a more complex picture – just as Vincent's own persona combined the analytical with the down-to-earth.

IN THE FRAME: THE VERDICT OF CONTEMPORARIES

In his reactions to other people's views of him, Vincent could sometimes be thick-skinned but at other times easily hurt. 'How preposterous it is to make oneself dependent on the opinion of others in what one does,' he wrote to Wil in mid-1888 (W4). Yet, on his tense return to his parents at Nuenen at the end of 1883, he had compared himself to a shaggy dog with wet paws and a loud bark, always getting in the way. Unlike the dog, however, Vincent was sensitive to what people thought of him.

What did Vincent look like in the eyes of his contemporaries? Testimony as to physical appearance can vary wildly, and descriptions of Van Gogh are no exception. P.C. Görlitz, Vincent's co-worker in the Blussé and van Braam bookshop in Dordrecht, remembered Vincent as well-built, with a face covered with freckles and red hair that stood straight up on end. This was Vincent in 1877, but in Paris in 1886 he struck the Scottish artist A.S. Hartrick as 'a rather weedy little man with pinched features' (quoted in Stein, S.A. (ed.)). However, Emile Bernard, also recalling those Paris days, said Vincent was of medium height and stocky, walking 'with an abrupt gait'. And Adeline Ravoux, the girl whom Vincent painted in Auvers in 1890, recalled him as of 'good size', with a 'very bright, soft and calm' look. There are also accounts of how Vincent looked after he had mutilated his left ear in December 1888. Paul Signac observed in the Spring of 1889 that Vincent still wore a protective bandage, while Adeline Ravoux remembered how Vincent's shoulder had become bent on that side. In a memoir written in 1956, she stated that Vincent neglected his appearance, and a fellow student at the Antwerp Academy (January–February 1886) named Hageman described Vincent as dishevelled. On the other hand, A.S. Hartrick denied this, asserting that Vincent dressed better than many at Cormon's studio.

Regarding Vincent's attire, Anton Kerssemakers, to whom Vincent gave art lessons in 1885, recalled Vincent's shaggy overcoat and fur cap (also noted in Paris by Gauguin, who added that Vincent's overcoat was of goatskin). At the Antwerp Academy, Hageman compared Vincent's blue smock to those 'worn by Flemish livestock merchants', while Adeline Ravoux brought to mind his short jacket in blue twill and a felt hat with wide brim (or straw hat in summer). Vincent, she noted disapprovingly, declined to wear a collar and tie.

Sadly, no photographs capturing the face of Vincent in mature adulthood have yet come to light. A photograph found among the papers of the Belgian artist Anna Boch, and purporting to show Vincent and Gauguin in late 1888, Gauguin's arm around Vincent's shoulder in a 'hail fellow well met!' pose, seems to be a spoof, with Anna's brother Eugène dressed up as Gauguin and a 'Van Gogh' unknown. Perhaps modern technology could be used to 'age' Vincent's youthful 1872 photograph and, by mixing in a computer synthesis of all Vincent's self-portraits, give us a good idea of what Van Gogh really looked like in his full maturity.

How did contemporaries perceive Vincent van Gogh as an individual and as an artist?

Theo van Gogh (1857–91)

It would be wrong to say that Vincent's debt to his brother brought with it any great sense of burden and obligation, since both Vincent and Theo rejected the definition of their 'paintings for money' arrangement as charity. Consistently, in his letters to his brother, Theo tells Vincent not to worry about the money he has sent him. Vincent's work and friendship are more valuable than Theo's money and he will not hear of Vincent returning any of it. However, Theo thought that Vincent spent too much on other people and he wanted Vincent to concentrate more on his own needs, 'at least until your budget balances better' (to Vincent, October 1888, T2). Theo sent regular money orders to Vincent at Arles and would ask Vincent to let him know by telegram if they fell short of his requirements.

To cover the cost of treatment and accommodation, Theo also sent monthly sums to Dr Peyron at the St-Rémy asylum, enclosing letters asking after Vincent's progress. In his letters to Vincent, Theo expresses deep anxiety when Vincent is passing through a crisis, 'this nightmare' (T14), over-exerting himself and risking an attack of vertigo or exposing himself to lead poisoning from paint, or to the effects of cold (which Vincent hated). Invitations to take a break at Theo's flat in the **Cité Pigalle** are frequent and Theo approached Camille Pissarro to contact 'worthy' Dr Gachet in Auvers, so that he might help Vincent should he return to the north. Despite these anxieties, Theo had faith in his brother, admiring his perseverance and courage. Theo was confident that Vincent would live to see success: 'It will come of its own accord by reason of your beautiful pictures' (to Vincent, January 1890, T25). Corot and Millet sold their work in the end – and so would Vincent.

KEYWORDS

Cité Pigalle: a quiet street to the south of Montmartre. Theo and Jo moved in to Apartment Number 8 in 1889.

Every Sunday (as Theo's wife Jo wrote to her 'brother' Vincent), Theo would enjoy rearranging his paintings in their flat. He propped up one of the *Sunflower* paintings on the sitting-room mantelpiece where it looked superb, like cloth finely embroidered with satin and gold.

Theo, a well-established art dealer, would note proudly how Vincent's work was progressing. There would be a new vigour in the colour; the 'epitome' of Vincent's thoughts more intensely conveyed; a greater clarity of expression and less glaring tones in the harmony, and always the reference to Vincent expressing truth and the purity of nature in his pictures.

From Theo, Vincent received regular reports of the views of other artists, for example the lithographer A. M. Lauzet who said that Vincent's paintings had 'the genuine character of Provence' (T25), and Paul Gauguin, who described Vincent's pictures at the Independents' show in March 1890 as the 'nail' on which the other exhibits hung (T29).

Theo's own references to Vincent were not always positive. There were quarrels over Vincent's strained relations with their parents, Anna and Dorus, and in 1887 he wrote of Vincent's exasperating behaviour in Paris. Theo's letters also had the ring of prophecy. As he wrote to Vincent in October 1888: 'So Gauguin is going to join you; it will mean a great change in your life' (T1). And in June 1890, with Vincent having less than a month and Theo less than a year to live: 'We shall have to battle all through life without eating the oats of charity they give to old horses in the mansions of the great. We shall draw the plough until our strength forsakes us, and we shall still look with admiration at the sun or the moon, according to the hour' (T39).

The Views of Other Artists

Both Anton Kerssemakers and Willem Wenkenbach, artist friends of Vincent in 1885, noted the speed with which Vincent painted. François Gauzi, friend and biographer of Toulouse-Lautrec, went so far as to refer to the 'disorderly fury' of Vincent's methods, and he described Vincent as using his brush like a shovel. In complete contrast, the Danish artist Johan Rohde perceived Vincent using his brush like a precision instrument, to reflect different angles of light.

Vincent's genius as a colourist has also been vividly recalled. A.S. Hartrick witnessed Vincent rolling his eyes and hissing through his teeth as with great relish he intoned the name of colours ('blue' ... 'orange') and placed the one complementary colour next to the other. Emile Bernard wrote that Vincent could make paintings 'sing' by placing a red one next to a green, and a blue one alongside a yellow. The German **Jugendstil** artist, August Endell, was in awe of Vincent's immense colour range and bold colour contrasts, and of his ability to 'speak with a strong voice without shouting'.

KEYWORDS

Jugendstil: 'Youth Style': the German form of Art Nouveau.

That Vincent used art as a language was understood by many artists, including the Spaniard Antonio Cristobal, who wrote that Vincent 'envisaged art as a language that addresses everyone, as a symbol, as a verb'. According to Emile Bernard, for Vincent painting was a kind of literature, written not in words but in colours and lines.

Although it was the belief of Emile Bernard that Vincent did not have a 'decisive' style until his Arles period (February 1888 to May 1889), other artists nevertheless paid tribute to the depth of Vincent's work. It was Gauguin who told Vincent, concerning the 1890 Independents' show, that in painting subjects from nature Vincent was the only exhibitor *'who thinks* there'. For the Dutchman J.J. Isaäcson, Vincent revealed afresh 'our domain, our earth, our heritage'. The generosity of spirit that Vincent conveyed through his art was acknowledged by the painter Richard Roland-Holst (1868–1938), pioneer of Van Gogh exhibitions in the Netherlands; he believed that Vincent painted so ruggedly and energetically because he wanted 'to give infinitely more than he was able to give.'

On the other hand, anecdotal evidence sometimes brings to light the darker side of Vincent's character. For example, A.S. Hartrick described how Vincent could be brutal in his 'put-downs' of artists whose work he thought poor. One such victim, the English artist Henry Ryland, was left a nervous wreck – although it did not prevent him exhibiting later at the Royal Academy. Willem Wenkenbach, a Dutch artist, recalled Vincent's strained relations with the upright bourgeoisie of Nuenen, and how, at the thought of these disagreeable encounters, Vincent would kick at his easel resentfully.

Nevertheless, for the Danish artist Johan Rohde, Vincent was one of the 'great European trailblazers', and for the German August Endell, he was 'a stimulator, a revolutionary, a pioneer, who shows mankind a thousand new paths … a happy premonition that out of our time, which so often seems tired and leaden and without hope and life, may yet arise new creativity and new courage'.

The Views of Writers

In an influential article, published six months before Van Gogh's death, the 25-year-old Albert Aurier wrote that Vincent's art was generated by 'Ideas'. For example, 'the sower' was a natural form but, at a deeper level, it was an Idea, namely 'the regenerator of life'. Vincent's art, Aurier expounded, was an art of the most exhilarating and ecstatic excess: Vincent painted 'flaming landscapes, like the effervescence of multicoloured enamels in some alchemist's diabolical crucible'. Vincent could express what he saw as an 'orgiastic extravagance' – an image echoed by the writer Maurice Beaubourg who wrote of Vincent's 'orgies of molten, golden tones'.

To the Belgian Ernest Closson, Vincent's painting *The Red Vineyard* (1888) conveyed 'the fermenting fumes and the intoxication, the mad passion and the effervescence of wine'. But if *The Red Vineyard* was, for Closson, a **Bacchanalian** experience, for the American critic Cecilia Waern, *A Path Through a Ravine* (1889) was like **Dante's *Inferno***. And the German art historian and early biographer of Van Gogh, Julius Meier-Gräfe, wrote memorably that Vincent 'did not paint his pictures: it was as if he exhaled them, in a gasping, boiling breath'. While Meier-Gräfe meant this as a compliment, the Basque writer Charles Merki wrote sarcastically that Vincent's

> **KEYWORDS**
>
> Bacchanalian: after Bacchus, the God of wine, evoking the spirit of drunken revelry.
>
> Dante's *Inferno*: the narrative poem by Dante Alighieri (1265–1321) that tells of his descent into Hell.

colour, 'so abundant and, in many places a few centimetres in height – has caused infatuation. How can one not believe in a practical joke?' The Dutchman Johan de Meester was more perceptive when he commented that Vincent always went 'one notch beyond' other painters – his 'darks' were darker than traditional Dutch paintings, his 'lights' brighter than the most colourful French ones. Beyond this, de Meester believed that there was a clear cultural politics at work in Vincent's art – that Vincent, convinced that art could stimulate the masses, strove for 'a broadening influence of art with a strongly democratic sense …'

For Maurice Beaubourg, Vincent was an 'intuitive rather than a scientific artist', whose art contained symbolic complexities 'wherein the least object, the least colour, represented an entire twelve-**canto** poem, suggesting an entire

KEYWORDS

Canto: the subdivision of a long poem.

philosophy'. But perhaps the last word should lie with the French writer Sévérin Faust, for whom Vincent 'appeared like a meteor and disappeared too soon'.

IN THE GALLERY: INSPIRING POSTERITY

Throw a stone into a pond. The ripples will radiate towards the outer edge, before the circles dwindle to nothing. This sequence of events, from first decisive impact to ever-weakening backwash, is the reverse of what happened when Vincent was presented to the world, after his death, by way of international exhibitions. Indeed, far from fading to the margins of cultural awareness, through such exhibitions the impact of Van Gogh's art became ever stronger. Even so, this process took time and was somewhat erratic in its progress. Controversy had dogged Vincent's art in his own time and critical debates continued; appreciation of his work was also subject to ongoing shifts in fashion, as various painters and their factions slid in and out of popularity.

Nevertheless, by the end of 1891 the first Van Gogh retrospective had opened in the Netherlands, appropriately in The Hague where Vincent had once studied the art of painting. Several important shows then followed, notably in Amsterdam, where Vincent's sister-in-law Johanna played a leading part in the organization. Moving further afield, a group of progressive Danish artists unleashed Vincent's work on Copenhagen in the first ever Van Gogh and Gauguin exhibition, held in 1893.

The 1890–2 exhibitions in Paris, following Vincent's death, were largely thanks to artist friends such as Signac and Bernard. However, it was the art dealer Vollard (often regarded as Theo van Gogh's 'successor') who kept the flame burning in France with three Van Gogh exhibitions at his Paris gallery in 1895–7. These shows can be seen as a bridge to the major Van Gogh retrospective (of 71 works), organized by the Bernheim-Jeune Gallery in Paris in 1901. It was this exhibition that so influenced Matisse, Derain and their colleagues later labelled the 'Fauves' (or 'Wild beasts') and would soon take Vincent's work to a much wider European audience. That same year it was the turn of Germany, when the contemporary art scene in Berlin was struck by **Secession's** showing of Vincent's work. The innovative gallery owner, Paul Cassirer, soon followed suit and Vincent's reputation in Germany was reinforced in 1905 by the first of three further exhibitions held by Cassirer. Indeed, by 1905 there was something of a Van Gogh 'cult' in Germany.

KEYWORDS

Secession: A group of artists rebelling against the official system of art exhibitions. The Berlin Secession was founded in 1899.

The same could not yet be said of Britain and America. In 1910–11, the artist and critic Roger Fry organized a high-profile exhibition in London, 'Manet and the Post-Impressionists', at which 21 Van Goghs were displayed – to a mixed reception. When 18 works by Vincent were displayed at New York's Armory Show in 1913 – America's first significant exposure to Van Gogh – the reaction was even more hostile. Nevertheless, by the early 1920s, both America and Britain had staged their first one-man Van Gogh exhibitions to critical acclaim, while in Japan, Vincent's reputation was also being consolidated.

* * *SUMMARY* * *

● Eyewitness descriptions of Vincent are contradictory and there are no photographic portraits of him as a mature adult.

● Vincent saw himself engaged on an artistic mission and he certainly had an exceptional creative drive. However, he was not insensitive to criticism.

● Theo's letters sought to boost Vincent's confidence by commenting on Vincent's progress and relaying encouragement from other artists.

● For understanding the impact that Vincent made, reviews and recollections by his contemporaries in art and literature are a rich resource.

● Thanks to pioneering exhibitions, Vincent's reputation was soon established in progressive circles as a deeply expressive innovator. Many others, however, took offence at his radicalism or what they saw as the crudity of his painting style.

7 Vincent's Influence on Other Artists

It goes without saying that influence can be short-lived and can vary in intensity, and it would be misleading to suggest that Vincent necessarily, if ever, had a 'permanent' influence on any artist. However, his art did much to 'inform' the styles of the 25 years before the First World War and was a catalyst to later generations of modernism. This chapter focuses on a selection of artists who, at one time or another, derived inspiration from Vincent van Gogh.

EDVARD MUNCH

Sadly perhaps, the paths of Edvard Munch (1863–1944) and Vincent van Gogh never actually crossed. Munch, the Norwegian Expressionist and painter of *The Scream* (1893), first visited Paris briefly in 1885, a year before Vincent's arrival, and by the time Munch returned to Paris to study painting in October 1889, Van Gogh was in the asylum of St-Rémy. Nevertheless, Munch would have encountered Vincent's paintings in Paris and later in Berlin, and the spiritual and stylistic paths of these pioneering artists most certainly did connect. Indeed, in later life Munch would reflect on his debt to the Dutch artist. As he wrote in October 1933, 'During his short life, Van Gogh did not allow his flame to go out. Fire and embers were his brushes during the few years of his life, whilst he burned out for his art. I have thought, and wished, that in the long term, with more money at my disposal than he had – to follow in his footsteps. Not to let my flame die out, and with burning brush, to paint to the very end' (quoted in Tøjner, P.J., *Munch in His Own Words*, Prestel, Munich & London, 2001).

There are poignant similarities in the lives of Van Gogh and Munch. Interestingly, they both decided to become painters in the same year, 1880. Both were to experience mental illness and both inflicted injury on themselves (Vincent slicing off part of an ear, Munch shooting himself in the hand). Vincent suffered his first serious 'crisis' in late 1888; Munch had a severe nervous breakdown in 1908. It was in the years following this trauma that Munch's art was particularly close to Vincent's, for example, in *The Sun* (1909–11), a radiant mural for Oslo University. But Munch's affinity with Vincent's art had already been affirmed, in deeply expressive paintings, such as *The Starlit Night* (1893) and *White Night* (1901). Both Munch and Vincent placed a high value on the role of spirituality in art and they believed that it was 'a sin against the spirit to produce anything by coldly rational means' (Hodin, J.P., *Edvard Munch*, Thames & Hudson, London, 1972, p.8).

While Munch did not meet Van Gogh, he did get to know Paul Gauguin in Paris (1893–5) and, just as Gauguin had been influenced by Vincent, so Munch in his turn was inspired by Gauguin, who, with Vincent, would play a significant part in forging the future direction of Munch's art.

PAUL GAUGUIN

Van Gogh and Gauguin lived and worked together in Arles from mid-October to late-December 1888. This period was cut short by their dramatic quarrel, although it had been Gauguin's original plan to stay until the following Spring.

With Gauguin's encouragement, Vincent took up, what was for him a difficult challenge, namely painting *de tête* (from memory) rather than directly from the model or motif. As Druick and Zegers have pointed out, this also involved a much slower method of working, in contrast to Vincent's normally high-speed technique. This new approach, at its height in November 1888, produced a highly distinctive group of paintings, including *A Memory of the Garden (Etten and Nuenen)*, *The Red Vineyard*, and *A Novel Reader*.

As intended, the 'learning' was a two-way process. For a time at least, Gauguin shared Vincent's interest in modern Naturalist authors such as Emile Zola, with their concern for social realism. The sleazy interior of Gauguin's *Night Café in Arles* (1888) is an obvious 'take' on Vincent's own *The Night Café* (1888). In some paintings, Gauguin was influenced also by Vincent's *impasto* technique, while the idea of incorporating a Vincent-type 'message' into his paintings became established. For example, in the same month that Vincent painted his own *Red Vineyard* (November 1888), Gauguin composed *Human Miseries*, an 'emblematic' painting about the grape harvest. It is rich in complex symbolism. A red vineyard climbs and descends through the picture space in the shape of a steep mountain, evoking the harvest's crushing toil. On the 'mountain' two peasant women bend and strain as they pick the interminable grapes. In the centre foreground, a seated female figure, head in hands, conveys a highly ambiguous message. Does she personify the exhaustion felt by all who toil at the harvest, no matter what consolation from the fruits of their labour? Or has she reaped her own bitter harvest – of temptation? If so, the darkly-hooded standing figure to the left, its hand in a pouch of grapes, might represent grief. Whatever the symbolism, agricultural themes (closely identified with Vincent) would be ones to which Gauguin too would return. This was also the case with portraiture, where Gauguin's interest was boosted by Vincent's enthusiasm for the genre.

Fundamentally, Vincent's 'Studio of the South' was, for Gauguin, a creative stepping-stone. In pursuit of an alternative artistic lifestyle, a 'Studio of the Tropics', Gauguin boarded a steamer bound for Polynesia in April 1891 and, for much of the rest of his life, he would remain there. His health was to suffer terribly, but in artistic terms he went on to sow and reap a fabulous harvest of richly symbolic paintings, just as Vincent had harvested the awesome power of nature in Provence and Auvers.

THE FAUVES

For the young avant-garde artists who became known as The Fauves (Wild Beasts) the Van Gogh retrospective at Bernheim-Jeune in Paris in March 1901 was an experience nothing short of an emotional earthquake. As André Derain, one of the Fauves' luminaries put it, 'It is almost a year now since we saw the Van Gogh exhibition, and really, the memory of it haunts me ceaselessly' (quoted in Saltzman, see Further Reading section). And Derain's colleague, Maurice de Vlaminck, noted Vincent's 'revolutionary, almost religious feeling in the interpretation of nature. I left this retrospective, my inner being deeply shaken' (quoted in Stein). Vlaminck saw in Vincent someone who had, in his portraits, arrived where Vlaminck himself wanted to be – tearing open his soul and displaying it in blazing colour. Indeed, in 1905 (the year of a subsequent Van Gogh retrospective and of the Fauves' own shocking début as a 'group'), Derain and Vlaminck painted wild-hued portraits of each other that were a revelation.

In conversation with Gaston Diehl in 1945, Henri Matisse (the leader of the Fauves) said that Vincent had been crucial in 'the rehabilitation of the role of colour, and the restitution of its emotive power' (Flam, J., *Matisse on Art*, Phaidon, Oxford, 1973/8, p.98). It was Matisse who helped to organize the 1905 exhibition of Vincent's work and who, in his 1905 portrait of his wife, with its infamous green stripe travelling vertically through Amélie's face, seemed, like Vincent himself, to be attacking the canvas with his emotions.

PABLO PICASSO

It may seem odd to connect Picasso, the great advocate of **Cubism**, with Vincent van Gogh. However, there are indeed some significant points of contact.

> **KEYWORD**
>
> Cubism: based on the cube, sphere, cone and cylinder, this style sought to represent different facets of a subject simultaneously, to reveal further dimensions.

* Picasso's *Mother and Child* (1901),with a baby sitting on its mother's lap, relates to Vincent's Arles painting of Augustine Roulin with her baby, Marcelle (1888) in its colour and composition. Picasso would have seen this painting in Vollard's Paris gallery.

* Picasso liked to paint, in his words, 'all at one go like Van Gogh'. An example is his *Nudes in the Forest* (1907–8).

* Picasso's self-portraits of 1907 show how he had assimilated the intensity of Vincent's own self-portraits.

* In the last stages of Cubism (c.1912–14), as John Richardson has suggested, Picasso (then in the South of France) lightened his palette just as Van Gogh had done.

* Through Vincent's example, Picasso's art was released from conventional restraints and became more uninhibited.

* As Picasso himself acknowledged, Vincent, in expressing the truth of nature by looking below its surface appearance, reached beyond nature itself and in the process made himself independent of it. Through Cubism, Picasso too arrived at a new vision and understanding of the subjects he portrayed.

THE GERMAN EXPRESSIONISTS

The first substantial Van Gogh exhibition in Germany opened in December 1901. It was organized by the Berlin gallery owner Paul Cassirer (who had been inspired by his visit to the Van Gogh retrospective at Bernheim-Jeune in Paris earlier that year). Such was its impact, that by 1914, German collections had more Van Goghs than anywhere else outside the Netherlands. Indeed, from that point, Vincent's art became crucial to the development of painting in Northern Europe, wielding an influence deeper perhaps than that of Gauguin or Cézanne (Rishel & Sachs, see Further Reading section).

Among those inspired by Vincent's art in the years before the First World War, were the two main Expressionist groups in Germany: Die Brücke (The Bridge), founded in 1905, and the more international and less cohesive Der Blaue Reiter (The Blue Rider), which first exhibited in 1911.

Die Brücke

At the end of 1905, a later Van Gogh exhibition organized by Cassirer reached Dresden. Among its visitors were some former architectural students who were already calling themselves 'Die Brücke' and whose goal was artistic freedom from the 'Establishment'. As the 1905 manifesto of their leading figure Ernst-Ludwig Kirchner expressed it – in words with which Vincent would have empathized – 'Everyone who reveals his creative drives with authority and directness belongs to us' (Hughes, R., *The Shock of the New*, London, 2nd edition, 1991, p.286). The strong impact that Vincent's art had on Die Brücke is shown in a series of self-portraits painted by members of the group between 1906 and 1907, most notably by Karl Schmidt-Rottluff, the youngest of the group. In *Self-Portrait* (1906), an agitated blue background rises up like a vertical sea, while the slashes of red, orange, yellow, blue and green that make up the face, reveal the artist's determination to break free of conventional form.

Der Blaue Reiter

By 1912, Vincent's influence was reaching out to the modernist art world of Munich and particularly to members of Der Blaue Reiter, the loosely organized group of Expressionists formed in Germany in 1911. Der Blaue Reiter aimed to reach 'behind the veil of appearances'. Vincent made a deep impression on the famous painter of the 'soul' of horses and tigers, Franz Marc (1880–1916). Marc, like Vincent, had been a student of theology. The Swiss Paul Klee (1879–1940), who exhibited with Der Blaue Reiter in Munich, found inspiration in Vincent's use of line to create a unified pictorial structure. A Russian member of the Group, David Burliuk (1882–1967), also a leader of the **Rayonists**, described Vincent as 'nearly universal in his short-time attempt to reflect the conglomerate facets of life', and therefore more significant than either Gauguin or Cézanne (quoted in Stein).

> **KEYWORD**
>
> Rayonists: influenced by Italian Futurism, they were abstract and semi-abstract painters who represented dynamic movement via energetic lines and vigorous colour.

An Austrian exhibitor with Der Blaue Reiter was Oskar Kokoschka (1886–1980). He had seen Vincent's intense and probing portraits, with their expressive colour and searching line, at an exhibition in 1906. Kokoschka was traumatized by the experience, yet felt inspired to paint his own series of psychological studies, the 'Black Portraits'. For example, in a process that parallels the psychoanalysis then fashionable in Vienna, Kokoschka 'dissected' the controversial Viennese architect Adolf Loos, revealing the tensions and strains of his character.

Oskar Kokoschka and Vincent van Gogh suffered the same fate in the 1930s. Because of the Nazis' campaign against 'degenerate art', their paintings were removed from galleries throughout Germany and, after the German invasion in March 1938, from those in Austria too. In September 1938, Kokoschka left for England and for a time painted watercolours on the Cornish coast.

GILMAN AND BACON

The British artist most memorably influenced by Van Gogh was Harold Gilman (1876–1919). With the more famous Walter Sickert, Gilman was one of the founders of the Post-Impressionist Camden Town Group that exhibited scenes of urban life. Gilman was mesmerized by the Van Goghs at the *Manet and the Post-Impressionists* Exhibition (1910–11) and by those he saw at the Bernheim-Jeune Gallery, also in 1911. Van Gogh became Gilman's hero and Gilman would dedicate his paintings to him, first bowing to a reproduction of Vincent's self-portrait with pipe and bandaged ear, then proposing the toast: 'A toi [To You], Van Gogh!' (Lilly, M., *Sickert: The Painter and His Circle*, Elek, London, 1971, p.130).

Many of Harold Gilman's paintings relate directly to Van Gogh precedents. *The Canal Bridge, Flekkefjord* (c.1913), which Gilman painted in Norway, is a synthesis of Vincent's *Bridge at Asnières* (1887) and *The Langlois Bridge at Arles* (1888). Gilman's composition of *Tea in a Bedsitter* (1916) includes, in homage to Gilman's hero, an empty rush-seated chair, somewhat reminiscent of *Van Gogh's Chair* (1888).

Gilman's painting of his charlady Mrs Mounter, *Sitting at the breakfast table* (1917), is Van Gogh's *Woman at a Table in the Café du Tambourin* (1887), *L'Arlésienne*, and *Postman Roulin* (both 1888), all rolled into one. Like a hound after truffles, Gilman rooted out Vincent's paintings. He also devoured Vincent's letters, a selection of which had their first English publication in 1912.

As his fellow artist Marjorie Lilly recalled, Harold Gilman spent so much money on painting materials, rather than food, that he became malnourished and died in the influenza epidemic of 1919. But whereas his association with Van Gogh had, until his fatal illness, been a happy one, the same cannot be said of the painter Francis Bacon (1909–92). Perhaps predictably, Bacon's 'take' on Van Gogh is grim in the extreme. His *Studies for Portrait of Van Gogh*, first shown in 1957, are eight garish variants on Vincent's jaunty *Artist on the Road to Tarascon* (1888). In Bacon's *Studies*, Vincent's original expression of keen anticipation of a creative day ahead is altered to one of tortured loneliness. Fields of red and orange (the same background colours found in Vincent's self-portrait with bandaged ear and pipe) traverse the composition of the fifth *Study*. The sky seems to be raining blood. Bacon's Van Gogh pauses on his tragic journey and turns his face towards the viewer – it is the face of death. Bacon adds 'bloodstains' to Vincent's chest and legs, and portrays his feet as swollen from life's tough pilgrimage. The animated shadow in Vincent's original painting is transformed into an ominous black shape, a symbol of the artist's fate.

TOOROP AND MONDRIAN

Since it was in the Netherlands that Vincent started out on his pilgrimage through life, a fitting place to conclude this chapter is 'where it all began'. The examples of two Dutch artists, Jan Toorop and Piet Mondrian, serve to illustrate the point that Vincent could wield a strong influence on other artists, without dictating their longer-term development.

In the early 1890s, Jan Toorop (1858–1928) was influenced by Vincent's expressive brushwork and vibrant colour contrasts, for example, in his paintings of the Surrey countryside (Toorop's wife was English). By this time, Toorop was also moving towards a highly personal form of Symbolism, in part derived from Javanese art. No doubt Vincent's own interest in the use of symbols was one of the factors that led Toorop to organize the first major Van Gogh exhibition in the Netherlands (in May 1892 at the **Kunstkring** in The Hague).

Just as Vincent had painted the dunes and fisherfolk at Scheveningen when studying art in The Hague (1882–3), so Jan Toorop twice made visits to the fishing village of Katwijk, further up the Dutch coast (1890–2, 1899–1904) in his eager quest for new subject matter and ideas. He painted the life of the shell-fishers there and, during his second stay, drew farmers from the region in a style reminiscent of Vincent's Nuenen phase of 1883–5.

KEYWORDS

Kunstkring: 'Art Circle': an association of avant-garde (ultra-modern) artists in The Hague.

Rosicrucianism: a sect claiming to know the secrets of nature and who practised alchemy. The Salon of the Rose + Cross was a Symbolist society to which some avant-garde artists belonged.

Like Van Gogh and Mondrian, Jan Toorop had a deep interest in religion. For a time he was interested in **Rosicrucianism**, but in 1905 he became a Roman Catholic. This conversion led to a new artistic focus on religious themes and, in stylistic terms, it also marked a return to the Pointillist style of Georges Seurat.

Like Vincent, Piet Mondrian (1872–1944) was taught art by a member of his family – in his case his Uncle Frits. But it was his two visits to North Brabant, Vincent's homeland, that led to an 'opening up' of Mondrian's art. His paintings of Brabant farmyards are, like Toorop's later drawings from Katwijk, reminiscent of Vincent's Nuenen pictures and they reveal an interest in formal structure. This interest would help to define Mondrian's celebrated geometric paintings of the 1920s to 1940s.

The pure colour of Mondrian's paintings such as *The Red Tree* (1908–10) and *Dune III* (1909) reveal Vincent's influence, while *Night Landscape* (c.1907/8) has Van Gogh-esque haloes around the stars. However, as with Toorop, the period before the First World War was one of rapid transformation for Mondrian. By 1912 he had also passed through Symbolism (using a Pointillist style called 'Luminism') and was beginning to explore a personal form of Cubism.

✷ ✷ ✷ *SUMMARY* ✷ ✷ ✷

● The Norwegian Edvard Munch felt deeply indebted to Vincent's expressive and personal style.

● Paul Gauguin's development as a Symbolist artist from 1889 was influenced by his collaboration with Vincent in Arles, as was his idea of a 'Studio of the Tropics'.

● The radical French artists, the Fauves, connected strongly with Vincent's revolutionary sense of colour.

● Picasso admired Vincent's ability to probe beneath nature's surface appearance. Where Vincent expressed 'soul', Picasso analysed 'structure'.

● Vincent's embodiment of artistic freedom and his engagement with the 'spirit of things' inspired the Expressionist movement in Germany.

● Whereas Harold Gilman embraced the positive spirit of Vincent's art, Francis Bacon interpreted Vincent's journey through life as a nightmare.

● Jan Toorop shared Vincent's interest in symbols. Piet Mondrian connected with Vincent in his early paintings of rural subjects. Mondrian's increasingly 'structural' approach led him towards geometric abstraction. Would Vincent have moved towards *expressive* abstraction had he lived?

The Van Gogh Phenomenon 1950–2000

IMAGES OF VAN GOGH

Film

Had artists been awarded Oscars, then Van Gogh would have been a strong contender: Most Vibrant Landscape (*Harvest at La Crau*, 1888); Most Penetrating Self-Portrait (from St-Rémy, 1889); Most Compelling Remake (*The Good Samaritan*, after Delacroix, 1890). But in 1956, Kirk Douglas, the fictional 'Van Gogh', lost out to Oscar winner 'Gauguin' (Anthony Quinn, Best Supporting Actor) when they starred in *Lust for Life*. Based on Irving Stone's hugely successful 1934 novel, and premiered at New York's Metropolitan Museum of Art, *Lust for Life* charts the battle of wills between Vincent and Gauguin. However, it is Vincent's other struggles that provide the film's most haunting images: his ardent promotion of the gospel thwarted by the apathy of the miners in the Borinage; his skirmishes with a flock of crows in the field of Auvers; and his inner struggle as he moodily drinks absinth in the Café de la Gare (the subject of *The Night Café*, 1888).

In 1972, the actor Michael Gough 'became' Van Gogh and downed turpentine in Mai Zetterling's superbly shot *Vincent the Dutchman*. True to its subject, this film (made for BBC television) bursts with brilliant images: Vincent drawing on his pipe as he strides to work past peach trees in full bloom; Vincent with lighted candles strapped to his hat as he makes a painting of the town of Arles at night; and, most affecting of all, Vincent with bandaged ear, sitting head in hand and shutting out the world, in the same pose as the old man he portrayed in *At Eternity's Gate* (1890).

In *Vincent the Dutchman*, Michael Gough speaks lines from Vincent's letters and these same letters, gems of autobiography, formed the core of a film from 1987, Paul Cox's *Vincent: the Life and Death of Vincent van Gogh*. On its triumphant opening in New York, film critic Andrew Sarris declared that it was 'the most profound exploration of an artist's soul ever to be put on film' (in *The Village Voice* newspaper, New York, quoted by Brian Case in *Time Out* magazine, 19–26 October 1988). *Vincent* was Dutch-born Cox's contribution (Director, Script, Photography, Editing) to the centenary of Van Gogh's death, which fell in 1990.

1990 saw at least two portrayals of the artist on film. Director Robert Altman offered an intense and convincing characterization in *Vincent and Theo*, starring Tim Roth and Paul Rhys; and, shining from Kurosawa's otherwise overstretched *Dreams* is a 'Van Gogh' sequence where some inspired special effects allow a Japanese artist to inhabit life-size recreations of Vincent's paintings, as he follows Van Gogh (Martin Scorsese) through the landscape.

Former artist Maurice Pialat's *Van Gogh* (1991) explored the last weeks of Vincent's life in Auvers and managed to 'paint' scenes cinematically, and the BBC's 1991 Omnibus *Van Gogh*, starring Linus Roache as Vincent and Anna Cropper as Vincent's mother Anna, used flashbacks and repetition to underscore the tragedy and pain of Vincent's life. At one point in the film, Vincent's concept of nature collides with Gauguin's vision. Scriptwriter Patrick Barlow has Gauguin ask of Vincent, 'What about the things you *can't* see? ... In the centre of nature, everywhere ... There are ghosts, there are spirits, that can't be seen but are there just the same ... There are worlds *within* worlds, Vincent, mysteries *within* mysteries' (from P. Barlow's script of *Vincent The Dutchman*, BBC Television, 1972). As Vincent wrote generously to Theo in late 1888, 'Gauguin gives me the courage to imagine things' (L562).

Perhaps one of the most rewarding films about Vincent is the Metropolitan Museum of Art's 1984 documentary, *In a Brilliant Light: Van Gogh in Arles*, which accompanied the Museum's exhibition of that title. Featuring extensive analysis by Van Gogh scholar, Ronald Pickvance, and some memorable comments from **John Rewald**, the film offers astounding close-ups in raking light, notably of *The Night Café* (1888), to show how perfectly each, apparently hasty, brushstroke sculpted its subject in paint. Most inspired is Pickvance's comment that in *Sunflowers* one image becomes many, the group of sunflowers are themselves symbolic of the artists' colony that Vincent hoped to found in the South of France.

> **KEYWORD**
>
> John Rewald (1912–94): one of the foremost experts on Impressionism and Post-Impressionism. Rewald was a consultant to the Van Gogh film *Lust for Life* (1956).

Sadly, there is no motion picture footage of Vincent himself; unlike Degas, Monet and Renoir, he died before the advent of moving film. In any case, given his intensely private nature, it is questionable that he would have consented. Nevertheless, Vincent's presence lives on through his paintings, still communicating intensely with his fellow person. As Michael Gough remarked in the BBC's 1972 film *Vincent the Dutchman*, 'There are few people in the West who are not influenced in their way of looking at the world around them by the way Van Gogh saw it. That is why, whenever we can, we celebrate him' (from the script of *Vincent the Dutchman*). Now, as much as ever, Vincent fires the human imagination.

Music

For those lucky enough to 'hear' colours, *The Starry Night* (1889) might indeed summon up the music of the spheres. However, any connection between Vincent and music, begins with the artist himself. Music was an art form in which he was deeply interested and he sought colour equivalents to the notes of the musical scale. As a listener he greatly admired the music of **Wagner**, while as a practitioner he took piano and singing lessons

> **KEYWORDS**
>
> Richard Wagner (1813–83): German composer whose music of myths and legends Symbolist artists perceived as a new art form.

and he also loved to sing English hymns. Vincent made sketches of musicians in Paris theatres and, in a domestic setting, painted Dr Gachet's daughter at the piano; the arpeggios she plays are echoed in the flowing contours of her dress.

Nearly a century later in 1971, the American singer Don McLean released the song 'Vincent', its famous lyrics inspired by his response to the painting *The Starry Night*. 'Vincent' reached Number 1 in the UK and Number 12 in the US charts, and it became an international gold disc – its success as glittering as the stars in *The Starry Night* itself. Fast forward 20 years, and bands named Go Van Gogh and blue van gogh are performing. Among the latter's songs is 'Sunflower Girl'. In 1957, 40 years before blue van gogh's debut CD, came a Turkish opera about Van Gogh by the little-known composer Nevit Kondalli.

The relationship between Vincent, Gauguin and the Café proprietress, Marie Ginoux (*L'Arlésienne*), has been explored in *Poet's Garden*, a musical by John Allee and Gary Matanky set in Arles in 1888. The musical was highly acclaimed on its opening in the US in 2001.

Advertising

In March 1987, following the £24,750,000 sale of *Sunflowers*, margarine advertisements appeared featuring Van Gogh's painting as a symbol of healthy living. Ironically, during his adult life Vincent himself rarely enjoyed good health. From Antwerp in February 1886 he wrote to Theo that for a year he had eaten hardly anything but bread – which makes the aforementioned adverts somewhat ironic. Not only have Vincent's images been appropriated for advertisements, but also for television commercials, packaging (wine, tea, potatoes and matchbox labels), and clothes (ties and T-shirts).

BUYING VAN GOGH: THE GREAT AUCTION SALES

When, in 1891, the French art critic Octave Mirbeau bought the late Vincent van Gogh's painting *Irises*, he paid a paltry 230 francs for it. Far into the future, in 1984, the Australian art critic Robert Hughes wrote,

'Dealers tell us that the day of the $10 million painting is at hand' (R. Hughes, 'Art and Money' in *Nothing If Not Critical*, London: Harvill/HarperCollins, 1987, p.389). And so it was to prove. The following year, *Wheat Field with a Rising Sun* (1889) climbed to $9.9 million at auction. Two years later, in March 1987, a version of *Sunflowers* was bought by the Japanese Yasuda insurance company for $39.9 million. Only eight months after that, Yasuda were blown out of the water when Alan Bond, an Australian brewing magnate, snapped up *Irises* for $53.9 million. Clearly, the 230 francs paid by Octave Mirbeau had been a bargain.

Between 1980 and 1987 the price of a Van Gogh increased ten-fold, with speculators inflating prices and basking in the prestigious acquisition of high-profile art. Indeed, as the mind-boggling sales of 1990 were to show, thanks to cheap borrowing and a strong yen, Japan was able to afford ever more astronomical sums for Van Gogh's work. In May 1990, the paper millionaire Ryoei Saito spent $82.5 million on the *Portrait of Dr. Gachet*, 1890 (the version with two books on Dr Gachet's table). The fact that Vincent portrayed Gachet wearing an infinitely sad expression (the 'heartbroken expression of our time'), and that the doctor himself was a socialist with altruistic aims, adds a layer of irony to the fate of his portrait. As Robert Hughes so trenchantly put it in his article 'The Decline of the City of Mahagonny', 'The new relations between "price" and "value" were … pushed from obscenity into farce in the Spring of 1990 when one Japanese investor paid $160.2 million for a Van Gogh and a Renoir'. Although the Japanese bubble burst in 1991, this was not the end of the story, for Van Gogh's own 'clean shaven' self-portrait sold in November 1998 for $65 million at Christie's in New York. The 'crazy years' were back again.

DOUBTS, DISCOVERIES AND THEORIES

Doubts

In the late 1990s, *The Art Newspaper* undertook far-reaching investigations into the question of Van Gogh forgeries. Its 1997 survey concluded that over 100 works were open to question. In 1998, focusing on public collections alone, *The Art Newspaper* named 18 pictures as fakes or of questionable attribution. Thanks to the co-operative efforts of museums and scholars to get to the truth, many were withdrawn from display or at least re-described.

However, the version of *Dr. Gachet* (1890) in the Musée d'Orsay was and is still in place. Accusations had been made that Gachet (who in this version leans on a table *without* books) had painted it himself. It was, therefore, subjected to detailed analysis by the French Museum Research Laboratory in Paris. Not only was the brushwork, in its strength and agility, shown to be authentically 'Van Gogh', but the red lake pigment that had been mixed with ultramarine for the foxglove flowers Gachet is holding, was shown to have faded – as it had in the undoubtedly genuine 'with books' version. Thus on both counts – brushwork and pigment – the Orsay's own *Dr. Gachet* was held to be authentic.

Such tests were anticipated for the 'Yasuda' *Sunflowers* (named, with no little satire, after the Japanese insurance company that bought it in 1987). This work led to fierce debate between champions and doubters; even the latter could not agree among themselves. In 1998, Ben Landais, a French devotee of Van Gogh, argued that it was painted by the Alsatian artist, Claude-Emile Schuffenecker, who had copied the original when he was restoring it in 1900–1. Even more sensationally, in 2001 the Italian Antonio de Robertis claimed it was in fact painted by Gauguin, who had secretly borrowed an original version from Vincent and reproduced it. In Japan, Holland and the UK, the possibility was discussed, of analyzing the 'Yasuda' *Sunflowers* alongside the *Sunflowers* belonging to The National Gallery in London, in order to reach a definite conclusion about the former's authenticity. Not since the Shroud of Turin had a work of art been so mired in controversy. In fact, Louis van Tilborgh and Ella Hendriks, writing in the December 2001 edition of the Van Gogh Museum *Journal*, have offered compelling evidence for the Yasuda *Sunflowers'* authenticity. And, thanks to the 2001–2 *Van Gogh and Gauguin: the Studio of the South* exhibition (see below), the Van Gogh Museum, National Gallery (London) and Yasuda versions of *Sunflowers* could at last be analysed alongside each other and significant similarities noted.

The question of fake Van Goghs goes back at least to the late 1920s, when the German art dealer Otto Wacker was jailed for fraud after trying to pass off his own fakes at a Van Gogh exhibition in Berlin. The son of the expert who exposed Wacker, Walter Feilchenfeldt, is now a leading scholar in this difficult field, along with Roland Dorn from Germany and Liesbeth Heenk from Holland. These experts base their conclusions, in part, on materials, technique and style, for example citing canvas or paper types and brush or pencil strokes as determinants of authenticity or forgery. But provenance (the known history of the picture) can also be crucial. Nonetheless, the provenance may be sound but the style wrong! Predictably, arguments 'for' and 'against' continue to rage.

Discoveries

Since the 1980s, 14 'new' Van Goghs have been catalogued, after emerging mainly from private collections. These include six oil paintings and three watercolours. Some were done in Holland, others in France and among them are a drawing of Vincent's girlfriend Sien, landscapes and still lifes. In late 2001, a study by Vincent of Paul Gauguin, in red beret and painting a yellow picture, was finally authenticated. However, it was a small painting of a bouquet of autumn flowers that proved to be Vincent's special gift to posterity. Bought in a Paris flea market after the Second World War, it emerged from an attic in 1995, unvarnished, unframed, unrestored, and unknown to art historians: the quintessential discovery.

Other paintings were known to exist but had disappeared. It was in 1991 that the journal *Artnews* broke the story of Soviet 'Trophy Art'. In revenge for similar thefts by German troops on Russian soil, Stalin's 'Trophy Brigades' had looted 2 million objects from German art collections at the end of the Second World War. Among the 98 French paintings looted from the estate of Otto Krebs, an industrialist, was Vincent's most brilliantly coloured rural scene, *Landscape with House and Ploughman* (1889). Fifty years later it emerged from a vault in the Hermitage, along with Vincent's portrait of Madame Trebuc, and so it was brought to light again in the West (with a preview in the March 1995 issue of *Vanity Fair*).

The theme of discovery also applies to the identification of locations – places associated with Vincent that have been pinpointed by amateur sleuths, historians and journalists. In the early 1970s, a postman named Paul Chalcroft researched the name Loyer (Vincent's landlady's name) from birth, marriage and census records and discovered that Vincent's address in Brixton was 87, Hackford Road. Soon afterwards, a journalist named Kenneth Wilkie located Vincent's own drawing of that house. In the mid-1950s, a local historian, William Johnson, researched parish records to find where Vincent's sister Anna had lived in Welwyn, Hertfordshire. In 1982, Ruth Brown, through studying Vincent's letters and old rates books, deduced where Vincent himself had lived in Ramsgate, Kent. The sum total of our knowledge of Vincent had increased and art historian Martin Bailey took things further when he was one of the first people in recent times to study the 'closed' Van Gogh family correspondence in the vaults of the Van Gogh Museum. Bailey wrote up his findings in *Young Vincent: the Story of Van Gogh's Years in England,* which was published in 1990.

Theories
The attitude of critics during Vincent's own time was looked at in Chapter 6, but how have more recent art historians viewed him?

As the art historian Cynthia Saltzman has explained, in the post-Second World War period it was the 'formalists' led by the American Clement Greenberg, who held sway. As their name suggests, they believed that form and style, not meaning, were all-important and that style had aesthetic value if it was true to the two-dimensional surface of the canvas; brushwork should, therefore, respect that surface. On that basis, Van Gogh, with his expressive sculptural *impasto*, was a problem. What was worse, he had made it all too clear that the *meaning* of his works was crucial to him.

By the late 1970s, these style-orientated formalists were under siege from a younger generation of subject-orientated art historians. In contrast to the formalists, the latter have been concerned with meaning and motivation. For example, at the opposite ends of the 1980s, Griselda Pollock and Linda Nochlin wrote challenging new analyses of Van Gogh. For Pollock, Van Gogh's concerns were explained by his bourgeois background and desire for commercial success, whereas for Nochlin, Vincent was just like the magazine illustrators and documentary photographers of the time – a socially concerned 'art worker'. Other historians studied the signs and symbols ('semiotics') in specific paintings, such as the 'with books' portrait of Dr Gachet. Why did Vincent paint those particular modern novels, *Manette Solomon* and *Germaine Lacerteux* by Jules and Edmond Concourt, on the table? Exactly which paintings by other artists inspired Vincent to give Gachet his melancholic pose and facial expression? What does the similarity between the portrait pose of Dr Gachet and that of *L'Arlésienne* signify?

On another level, scholars have reached for new insights into Van Gogh by studying his work in relation to the regions where he worked. In the late 1960s, experts from The Netherlands took the lead with their in-depth analysis of Vincent's 1880–5 'Dutch' period, reaching the conclusion that this was the decisive phase in his career. Vincent's under-researched Paris period (1886–8) was thoroughly examined in the 1970s by the Canadian scholar, Bogomila Welsh-Ovcharov. She followed her Doctorate from the University of Utrecht with a scholarly book on the subject, and then in 1981 curated the ground-breaking exhibition, *Vincent van Gogh and the Birth of Cloisonism*. Welsh's research recognized Vincent's true status at the forefront of the Parisian avant-garde. In the mid-1980s, it was the turn of the Arles, St-Rémy and Auvers periods (1888–90) to be held up to the spotlight. Ronald Pickvance's catalogues for two exhibitions, examining Vincent's work in the South of France (see below), underlined Vincent's stature as a first rank artist at the peak of his power – in Cynthia Saltzman's words, 'a consummate professional, producing at full throttle' (see Further Reading section). Roland Dorn, whose work on the Van Gogh forgeries question was discussed earlier, also played a key role in the study of Vincent's work in the South. Dorn concluded that the artist's work should be seen in terms of cycles: groups of work that were complementary or contrasting, in the same way that Vincent himself chose to hang his paintings in groups that went together or that made a decorative display pattern (he might place a portrait between two balancing landscapes of Provence, for example). Dorn also drew attention to Vincent's observation that reality had a 'multi-layered' quality, while for Ronald Pickvance, Vincent's paintings were 'defined groups and series ... organically connected' (quoted in Saltzman).

EXHIBITIONS AND BEQUESTS

Anniversary exhibitions

In 1953, the centenary of Vincent's birth, commemorative exhibitions were unveiled in The Netherlands at the Rijksmuseum and the Stedelijk Museum in Amsterdam (where, since 1930, the Van Gogh family collection had been on loan), and at the Kröller-Müller Museum in Otterlo. There was then no state Van Gogh Museum and it was not until the early 1960s that the *de Stijl* architect, Gerrit Rietveld (born

KEYWORD

De Stijl: Dutch word for 'the style'. The De Stijl artists practised a disciplined, economical form of pure abstraction based on laws that they believed were relevant to society. De Stijl's influential ideas about architecture and design were taught at the Bauhaus, the avant-garde college of art in Germany.

in 1888, the year Vincent moved to Arles), drew up sketches for one. These were further developed after Rietveld's death in 1964 and, in 1969, building work for the new museum began. In the presence of Vincent's nephew, Vincent Willem, the Rijksmuseum Vincent van Gogh was officially opened in 1973, with over 200 paintings and 500 drawings, a spectacular way to celebrate 120 years since Vincent's birth. The centenary of his death, in 1990, witnessed not only magnificent exhibitions in the Netherlands (Amsterdam and Otterlo), Germany and elsewhere, but also aptly-timed books, feature films and documentaries. Anticipating in 2003 the one hundred and fiftieth anniversary of Vincent's birth and the centenary of Gauguin's death, the exhibition *Van Gogh and Gauguin: The Studio of the South* opened in 2002 in the Van Gogh Museum in Amsterdam, having already drawn vast crowds at the Art Institute of Chicago. (See Further Reading concerning the exhibition catalogue.)

Ground-breaking themed exhibitions

Van Gogh and Gauguin: The Studio of the South, mentioned above, is an example of the sort of artistic 'frame' in which Vincent can be studied, each frame featuring a specific aspect of his life and career. In the 1980s, three exhibitions explored his years in France, two his Dutch period, and one his time in Belgium. An exhibition in 1992 focused on his years in England, one in 1995 on his Paris self-portraits, and another in 2001 on his drawings from Antwerp and Paris. (The latter featured a section on misattributions, explaining why certain drawings could not have been by Vincent.) An exhibition that travelled to Washington DC and Los Angeles in 1998–9, *Van Gogh's Van Goghs*, was very much an international show, covering his work in the Netherlands, Belgium and France. Other themed exhibitions examined Van Gogh's connections with specific artists and art movements, for example, *Van Gogh and Millet* (1989) and *Van Gogh and the Painters of the Petit Boulevard* (2001). Ever more focused research also produced innovative themes, such as *Van Gogh as Critic and Self-Critic* (1974), and *Cézanne to Van Gogh: The Collection of Dr. Gachet* (1999).

Between 1949 and 1954, Dr Gachet's son, Paul, and his wife Marguerite donated part of their own Van Gogh collection to the Musée D'Orsay, including some of Vincent's most celebrated works: the swirling *Self-Portrait* of September 1889; the 'without books' *Dr Gachet*, and versions of Vincent's *Bedroom at Arles* and *L'Arlésienne*.

Contemporary artists continue to pay tribute to Van Gogh through their own modernist styles. One example is Albert Ayme, a French artist whose earlier series included homages to the abstract artists, Mondrian and Malevich. In 1982, Ayme exhibited at Coutances in Normandy a sequence of large abstracts (each 1.75 m high by 1.2 m wide) entitled *Suite in Yellow, to the Glory of Van Gogh*. These ten variations on the colour of yellow, and its relations with the other primary colours red and blue, were triggered by a quote from one of Vincent's letters: 'It is true that to achieve the high yellow note I attained last summer, I really had to be pretty well keyed up' (L581).

'VINCENT IN THE NEWS'

To coin a phrase, Van Gogh makes great copy. More than any other artist, with the possible exception of Andy Warhol, Vincent is the subject of stories in the media. In 1998, *The Guardian* reported that the Pushkin Museum in Moscow was lending *Countryside around Auvers after the Rain* (1890) to the Auberge Ravoux (where Vincent had lived in Auvers, which is now a museum and research centre). The painting would be displayed behind bullet-proof glass and under a reinforced roof, thus finding itself sealed off from the very landscape that inspired it!

The first year of the true millennium yielded up four gems in particular. In March 2001, *The Guardian* ran a story relating how Astronomy Professor, Donald Olson, of West Texas State University had calculated the exact day and time that Vincent painted *White House at Night* (Auvers, 1890) by studying the position of Venus in the evening sky and the brightness of the sun on the roof. Gauguin featured in at least two stories: *The Sunday Times* told of a German art expert Rita Wildegans who had concluded that is was Gauguin who had cut off Vincent's left ear lobe with his sword, while *The Daily Telegraph* reported that an Italian student of Van Gogh believed that Gauguin was the painter of *Sunflowers*, bought in 1987 for over $50 million (see also 'Doubts, Discoveries and Theories' section).

Finally, to return to the photography which Van Gogh so disliked. In August 2001, *The Independent* highlighted new computer software developed at New York University which could analyse a digital photograph and turn it into the style of any artist, including Van Gogh. The Australian artist Rolf Harris, in a 2001 television programme, explored Vincent's style and invited amateur artists to paint sunflowers. However, although digitized 'translations' and attempts to paint in the Van Gogh style can be illuminating, they only serve to point to the uniqueness of the master. As Harold Gilman would say, 'A toi, Van Gogh!'

* * *SUMMARY* * *

- In film, narratives of Vincent's life and close-ups of his career show his lasting fascination as an artist and a man.

- Vincent's own love of music is echoed in popular songs and operas.

- In 1891, Octave Mirbeau paid 230 francs for *Irises*. In 1987, it cost Alan Bond $53.9 million.

- There is a debate about the authenticity of some Van Gogh pictures and, hitherto unknown 'Van Goghs', continue to emerge.

- Van Gogh scholars are finding new ways of looking at Van Gogh, as seen in innovative exhibitions of the artist's work.

- Over a century after the artist's death, Van Gogh stories are still a media 'industry'. No doubt, there is one being written at this very moment …

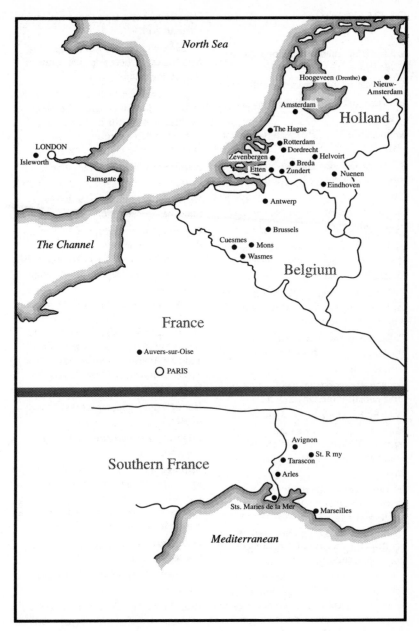

Van Gogh's Europe

GLOSSARY

Academician member of a prestigious Academy.

Aesthetics relating to a sense of beauty.

Altruism belief in living for the needs of others.

Avant-garde associated with the newest ideas.

Bacchanalian after Bacchus, the God of wine, evoking the spirit of drunken revelry.

Canon the recognized work of an artist.

Canto the subdivision of a long poem.

Cité Pigalle a quiet street to the south of Montmartre. Theo and Jo moved in to Apartment Number 8 in 1889.

Cloisonnists group of painters inspired by the structure and colour of medieval stained glass and enamel.

Collective co-operative association practising the principle of equality and mutual help.

Congregationalist a type of independent Protestant church.

Cubism based on the cube, sphere, cone and cylinder, this style sought to represent different facets of a subject simultaneously, to reveal further dimensions.

Dante's Inferno the narrative poem by Dante Alighieri (1265–1321) that tells of his descent into Hell.

De Stijl Dutch word for 'the style'. The De Stijl artists practised a disciplined, economical form of pure abstraction based on laws that they believed were relevant to society. De Stijl's influential ideas about architecture and design were taught at the Bauhaus, the *avant-garde* college of art in Germany.

Devotional texts texts concerned with religious faith.

En plein air recording or interpreting nature directly, in the open air rather than in the studio.

Expressionism art which is not 'strictly' realistic but could be said to be 'more truthful than the truth' (Van Gogh's phrase). It derives from the artist's emotional response to reality.

Fugitive not light-fast, i.e. prone to fading.

Genre type of subject – landscape, nude, battle scene, etc.

Goupil & Co. international firm of art dealers, later known as Boussod & Valadon. Vincent was employed in their branches in The Hague, London and Paris (1869–76).

The Hague School flourished between c.1860 and 1900. The group specialized in atmospheric landscapes and beach scenes but also painted views of town and city. Apart from Anton Mauve, the School also included Jozef Israëls ('the Dutch Millet').

Heliographic pictures created by early photography.

Impasto raised texture resulting from thick application of paint.

Impressionists artists who rebelled against traditional art and recorded rural and urban scenes with a new spontaneity, a freshness of colour and sensitivity to the effects of light.

Jesuitisms intrigues or equivocations ('necessary' lying).

Jugendstil 'Youth Style': the German form of Art Nouveau.

Kunstkring 'Art Circle': an association of avant-garde (ultra-modern) artists in The Hague.

La Mousmé originally a young Japanese girl.

Lithographs a design is drawn with greasy chalk on a flat stone which is then wetted. Because the printing ink is also greasy it will only print the greasy design and not the wet surrounding areas.

Lithographic stone stone onto which the design for a lithographic print is drawn.

Mistral violent wind in southern France.

Modernist the cutting-edge movements that made up the contemporary art scene.

Oeuvre body of work as a whole.

Old master Painter acknowledged as a master of art and usually working before 1800.

Orders classes of society.

Pendant a painting designed to complement another and to be hung next to it.

'Père' Tanguy a former member of the revolutionary Paris Commune (March–May 1871), who was a friend and supporter of many young artists.

Planes 'layers' in the composition of a picture, which lend depth from background to fore-ground.

Plasticity three-dimensionality, i.e. 'realness'.

Pointillists artists who applied colour in dots, say a blue next to a yellow which, when viewed from a certain distance, should mix to form green ('optical mixture').

Post-impressionist an artist pursuing a deeper or more strictly 'scientific' art than that practised by Renoir and his colleagues. Apart from Van Gogh, examples of Post-Impressionists include Gauguin, Seurat and Cézanne.

Rayonists influenced by Italian Futurism, they were abstract and semi-abstract painters who represented dynamic movement via energetic lines and vigorous colour.

Retrospective exhibition looking back on an artist's career.

John Rewald (1912–94) one of the foremost experts on Impressionism and Post-Impressionism. Rewald was a consultant to the Van Gogh film *Lust for Life* (1956).

Richepin Jean Richepin (1849–1926). Prolific French poet and author associated with the Chat Noir cabaret.

Rosicrucianism a sect claiming to know the secrets of nature and who practised alchemy. The Salon of the Rose + Cross was a Symbolist society to which some avant-garde artists belonged.

Secession A group of artists rebelling against the official system of art exhibitions. The Berlin Secession was founded in 1899.

Subliminal subconscious.

Symbolists painters whose style used colour, line and the subject itself to evoke ideas.

Richard Wagner (1813– 83) German composer whose music of myths and legends Symbolist artists perceived as a new art form.

Wood-engraving the wood-engraver takes a block of wood cut across the grain, and, using a sharp tool, makes the design by cutting away the non-printing areas to create a relief block. Wood-engraving was frequently used in the nineteenth century for illustrated books and magazines.

FURTHER READING

Letters and other primary sources

The Letters of Vincent van Gogh. Selected and edited by Ronald de Leeuw and translated by Arnold Pomerans, Penguin Classics, Harmondsworth, 1996.

The Complete Letters of Vincent van Gogh. Three Volumes. Edited by J. van Gogh-Bonger and V.W. van Gogh, translated by J. van Gogh-Bonger and C. de Dood, Thames and Hudson, London, 1958. Reprinted 2000.

Vincent by Himself. Edited by Bruce Bernard, Orbis, London, 1985.

Van Gogh: A Retrospective. Edited by Susan Alyson Stein, Könemann, Cologne, 1986.

Secondary sources on Van Gogh

Bailey, Martin, *Young Vincent: The Story of Van Gogh's Years in England,* W.H. Allen, London, 1990.

Dorn, Roland *et al., Van Gogh Face to Face: The Portraits,* Thames and Hudson, London, 2001.

Druick, Douglas W. and Zegers, Peter Karl *et al., Van Gogh and Gauguin: The Studio of the South,* Thames and Hudson, London, 2001.

Hammacher, A.M. & R., *Van Gogh: A Documentary Biography,* Macmillan, New York, 1982.

Kendall, Richard with Leighton, John and Van Heugten, Sjraar, *Van Gogh's Van Goghs,* National Gallery of Art, Washington DC, 1998.

Kōdera, T., *Vincent van Gogh: Christianity versus Nature,* John Benjamins, Amsterdam and Philadelphia, 1990.

McQuillan, Melissa, *Van Gogh*, Thames and Hudson, London, 1989.

Pabst, F. and Van Uitert, E., 'Notes from a Literary Life' in *Rijksmuseum Vincent van Gogh*, Van Uitert, E. (ed.) and Hoyle, M. (trans.), Meulenhoff/Landshoff, Amsterdam, 1987, pp. 75–84.

Rishel, J. and Sachs, K. 'The Modern Legacy of Van Gogh's Portraits' in Dorn *et al.*, *see above*.

Saltzman, Cynthia, *Portrait of Dr. Gachet: The Story of a Van Gogh Masterpiece*, Viking Books paperback edition, New York, 1999.

Sweetman, David, *The Love of Many Things: A Life of Vincent van Gogh*, Hodder & Stoughton, London, 1990.

CD-ROMS and Websites

The Complete Correspondence of Vincent and Theo van Gogh is available on CD-ROM via Bob Harrison at rgh@aeai.ca

The Complete Works of Vincent van Gogh are now available on CD-ROM via www.vangoghgallery.com. This site, supported by the Van Gogh Museum, has a wealth of interesting sections.

Gallery websites include:

www.vangoghmuseum.nl/
www.nga.gov/exhibitions/vgwel.htm (The Washington DC National Gallery of Art's *Van Gogh's Van Goghs* exhibition website.)

A starting point on Post-Impressionism is:
http://martyw.best.vwh.net.Postimpression.html

INDEX